They Also Taught in PARABLES

7.12

They Also Taught in PARABLES

RABBINIC PARABLES FROM THE FIRST CENTURIES OF THE CHRISTIAN ERA

Harvey K. McArthur & Robert M. Johnston

Academie Books Grand Rapids, Michigan
Zondervan Publishing House

THEY ALSO TAUGHT IN PARABLES
Copyright © 1990 by Harvey K. McArthur and Robert M. Johnston

ACADEMIE BOOKS is an imprint of Zondervan Publishing House,
1415 Lake Drive, S.E., Grand Rapids, Michigan 49506.

Library of Congress Cataloging-in-Publication Data

McArthur, Harvey K.
     They also taught in parables / Harvey K. McArthur and Robert M.
  Johnston.
        p.   cm.
     Includes bibliographical references.
     ISBN 0-310-51581-5
     1. Parables in rabbinical literature.   2. Jesus Christ–Parables.
  I. Johnston, Robert Morris, 1930-   . II. Title.
  BM518.P3M33   1990
  296.1'9–dc20
                                                                    89-28433
                                                                         CIP

#20564000

Unless otherwise noted, the Bible text is from the Revised Standard Version Bible, copyright 1946, 1952, 1971 by the Division of Christian Education of the National Council of the Churches of Christ in the USA, and is used by permission.

Translations of parables from The Fathers According to Rabbi Nathan, translated by Judah Goldin; The Midrash on Psalms, translated by William G. Braude; and Pesikta Rabbati, translated by William G. Braude are reprinted by permission of Yale University Press.

Parables from The Tosefta are reprinted by permission of KTAV Publishing House, Inc. and by the author, Professor Jacob Neusner.

Parables from The Mishnah, translated by H. Danby, 1933, are reprinted by permission of Oxford University Press.

Parables from The Midrash Rabbah, translated under the editorship of Rabbi Dr. H. Freedman and Maurice Simon; The Babylonian Talmud, translated under the editorship of Rabbi Dr. Isidore Epstein; and The Minor Tractates of the Talmud, translated under the editorship of the Rev. Dr. A. Cohen are reprinted by permission of Soncino Press.

Parables from Mekilta De-Rabbi Ishmael, translated by Jacob Z. Lauterbach and Pesikta De-Rab Kahana, translated by William G. Braude and Israel J. Kapstein are reprinted by permission of the Jewish Publication Society.

Edited by Leonard G. Goss and Craig Noll

Designed by Leonard G. Goss

Printed in the United States of America

90 91 92 93 94 95 96 / AK / 10 9 8 7 6 5 4 3 2 1

CONTENTS

FOREWORD

Perhaps there is no genre of biblical literature about which more has been written than the literary form "parable." This is partly understandable since over one-third of the teachings of Jesus is in the form of parables. However, more significantly, the frequent use and distinctive function of parables in Near Eastern literature are unparalleled in Western literature. Even our "local" imitations fall short of the dynamic and punch of these ancient parables. Hence, it is inevitable that such a huge body of literature has accumulated as scholars try to recover the genius and rhetorical effect of this genre of literature.

This problem is further complicated by the vexing question of the definition of a parable. An examination of the use of the term *parabolē* in the New Testament clearly shows that it includes many more figures of speech than the familiar and popular "story" parable. Basically, a parable involves a comparison—a feature or characteristic of something known is transferred explicitly or implicitly to something unknown. And it is precisely on this issue that parable interpretation in the twentieth century has been largely under the influence of A. Jülicher, who proposed that there can only be one point of comparison (*tertium comparationis*) in a parable. Hence, the other extreme, multiple *tertia comparationis*, ultimately resulting in allegory, must be avoided. In recent years the inadequacy of Jülicher's approach has been more and more recognized. This present study provides valuable data vis-à-vis this issue.

In the vast body of literature on parable interpretation very little consideration is given to the study of parables in rabbinic literature. Although in recent years greater attention is being given to the "Jewishness" of Jesus and the evangelists, nevertheless apart from an occasional allusion to a rabbinic parable, most authors neglect this area. Likewise, Paul Fiebig's ground-breaking study of rabbinic parables, published in the early 1900s in German and unfortunately not translated into English, receives scarce recognition in most studies on the parables of Jesus. As a result, this present study fills a troubling lacuna in the study of New Testament parables.

They Also Taught in Parables makes available for the first time in English a useful collection of parables from early rabbinic literature. This assemblage will be a valuable resource that no future study of New Testament parables can ignore and alone is worth many times the price of the book. The authors have carefully analyzed these parables in their context and cautiously dated them—thus avoiding the pitfall of much application of rabbinic literature to New Testament studies where the chronological problem is completely ignored.

Of equal value is the second part of this study where in ten essays the authors draw significant implications of their study of rabbinic parables for the interpretation of the parables of Jesus. In these discussions the authors display balanced judgment and are not given to extravagant claims. McArthur and Johnston have established the unique Palestinian setting of the parable genre and the numerous similarities in the parables of Jesus and of the rabbis. However, of interest is Jesus' distinctive use of parables to "shock" his hearers to reform and action—an important homiletical perspective for the present-day teacher and preacher. The overall results of this study clearly indicate that much of parable interpretation of the past decades must be qualified and redirected. The literary and rhetorical analyses to which parables have been subjected have been interesting, but some of these become irrelevant, given this better-defined *Sitz im Leben* of Jesus and his use of parables.

The authors are to be congratulated and commended for this contribution to the interpretation of the New Testament. Hopefully. this publication will provide an effective control over the speculative and wide-ranging interpretations of the parables of Jesus in recent years. It will certainly compel many to rethink and reevaluate some of the categories and presuppositions with which they have been working. Surely, the results of this study will be seen in future interpretations of and commentaries on the parables of Jesus.

Bastiaan Van Elderen
Vrije Universiteit, Amsterdam
Calvin Theological Seminary, Grand Rapids

INTRODUCTION

Western civilization has been permeated with at least a minimal knowledge of the Christian traditions, so that most people are aware that Jesus of Nazareth used parables as a favorite teaching device, and they would be able to identify parables such as The Prodigal Son or The Good Samaritan. In fact, a great many parables were attributed to Jesus; a standard work such as *The Parables of Jesus* by Joachim Jeremias (New York: Scribner, 1963) discusses forty parables from the Synoptic Gospels (Matthew, Mark, and Luke). The number could be slightly reduced or expanded, depending on one's definition of *parable*. While the later apocryphal gospels contain relatively few additional parables, an exception is the Coptic Gospel of Thomas discovered a few years ago. It attributes to Jesus numerous parables not previously known. The accuracy of this attribution is admittedly problematic, but at least it underlines the tradition that Jesus was a teacher of parables.

It is much less well known, except in Jewish circles or among specialists, that the Rabbis in the opening centuries of the Christian era also made extensive use of parables as a major teaching device. Raymond Pautrel estimated that the total number of parables in rabbinic literature is about 2,000 ("Les canons du Mashal rabbinique," *Recherches de science religieuse* 26 [1936]: 7). We have collected some 1,500 items from our own reading, and while this number includes repetitions in the various documents, our figures confirm that Pautrel's estimate is scarcely an exaggeration. Our own records include about 30 parables attributed to Simeon ben Yohai, a Rabbi from the middle of the second century of the Christian era; and a smaller but substantial number of parables are attributed to his contemporaries, Judah bar Ilai, Simeon ben Halafta, and Rabbi Meir. Traditionally Rabbi

Meir was regarded as a great teller of parables. The Babylonian Talmud says, "When R. Meir used to deliver his public discourses, a third was halakah [legal statements], a third haggadah [narrative or homiletic statements], and a third consisted of parables" (B. Sanhedrin 38b–39a); and again, "R. Meir had three hundred parables of foxes, and we have only three left." In addition, the Mishnah says, "When R. Meir died, there were no more makers of parables" (M. Sotah 9:5). Some question may be raised about the literal accuracy of these statements, and no doubt they reflect what has been called the exuberance of rabbinic writing, the tendency toward exaggeration for effect. Nevertheless, they do illustrate the prominence of parabolic language as a teaching device among the Rabbis (though this seems to have been more characteristic of Palestinian than of Babylonian Rabbis).

An entertaining incident is reported of the third-century Rabbi Bar Kappara. Rabbi Judah ha-Nasi had failed to invite him to a banquet celebrating the wedding of Judah's son—although all other Rabbis from the area had been invited. Embarrassed when he discovered this oversight, Judah promptly prepared another banquet, carefully including Bar Kappara among the invited guests. The host was astonished when the waiters took out the sumptuous courses to the guests but then returned shortly with the food untouched. When Rabbi Judah, who apparently was supervising the affair from the kitchen, asked the waiters what was happening, they explained that there was an old fellow at the table who, whenever a new course arrived, told some three hundred fox fables, which so fascinated the guests that they forgot to eat. Bar Kappara was having his revenge!

There was even a parable about the use of parables, addressed to any who might despise parables as unworthy of great scholars. Midrash Rabbah on the Song of Songs (1:1:8) records:

> Our Rabbis say: Let not a parable be lightly esteemed in your eyes, since by means of the parable a man can master the words of the Torah. If a king loses gold from his house or a precious pearl, does he not find it by means of a wick worth a farthing? So the parable should not be lightly esteemed in your eyes, since by means of a parable a man arrives at the true meaning of the words of Torah.

Here is a proof that it is so: for Solomon by means of the
parable penetrated to the finest nuances of the Torah.

Earlier in the same passage it states, in a graphic metaphor,
that Solomon made "handles to the Torah," that is, parables,
so that people would be able to grasp and comprehend it. All
may not agree that the writings alluded to (Proverbs,
Ecclesiastes, and the Song of Solomon) lead us into the most
profound understanding of the Torah, and the word *parable*
in this passage covers a wider range of figures than what we
would regard as parables, but the general point remains the
same.

Another indication of the popularity of parables is the
fact that occasionally in rabbinic literature a document begins
a parable and then breaks off without completing it. In such
cases the writer is apparently assuming that the readers
would be sufficiently familiar with the material to continue
the parable for themselves (see parable no. 49 in the
collection in part 1; see also Leviticus Rabbah 24:7 and
Deuteronomy Rabbah 4:4).

Parables are most numerous in the Midrash Rabbah on
Genesis and Exodus and in the Midrash on Psalms. In each
of these three there are at least 150 parables, although a
majority are not from the early rabbinic period and hence are
not included in this book.

This book is intended as a guidebook to the early
rabbinic parables, that is, the parables of the so-called
Tannaitic period, which ran from roughly the beginning of
the Christian era to between 200 and 220 C.E.* when Rabbi
Judah ha-Nasi brought to a conclusion the codification of
Jewish law in the document known as the Mishnah. (The
Rabbis writing during this period were the Tannaim [singu-
lar, Tanna]. The next period, between roughly 220 and 500
C.E., is known as the Amoraic period, or the time when the
Amora/Amoraim were active.)

Part 1 presents a substantial collection of these parables.
Earlier reference was made to the 1,500 items that we have in
our files of rabbinic parables. Of this number approximately
325 may, with some degree of probability, be attributed to
the early (or Tannaitic) Rabbis. These 325 are so identified
because they are either explicitly attributed to Rabbis of the

---

*C.E. (Common Era) is the religiously neutral equivalent of A.D. (Anno
Domini) and will be used throughout.

Tannaitic period or appear in documents that contain predominantly Tannaitic materials. All these parables are discussed in Johnston's dissertation, "Parabolic Interpretations Attributed to Tannaim" (Hartford Seminary Foundation, 1977). Here we consider only 125 parables, the last 10 of which (in an appendix to part 1) represent variants from the dominant parable form that is so conspicuous in these materials. The Rabbis perhaps would have been puzzled by our distinction between a "dominant parable form" and "variants," but for purposes of contemporary literary analysis the distinction may prove helpful.

The 115 regular parables in the present collection are arranged according to the documents in which they occur. Each document is introduced with preliminary comments, including the approximate number of parables in the document. The parables selected are numbered in sequence for handy reference in the chapters in part 2. If the parable is attributed to a specific Rabbi, his approximate date is given, and there are references indicating where doublets of a parable occur in the same or other documents. (Doublets are not repeated, but we do note any significant differences between the two. The principal character in one parable may be a man, for example, but in the doublet may be a king.)

Part 2 consists of ten chapters on various aspects of the parables. While the parables quoted in part 1 provide illustration of specific points, the chapters are based also on the evidence from the larger corpus of 325 parables found in Johnston's work, to which reference is made, as appropriate. Frequently there are references to still other rabbinic parables that come presumably from after the Tannaitic period. Since some readers will be familiar with the parables in the Gospels of the New Testament, there are isolated references to these by way of comparison. The bulk of the discussion involving New Testament parables is concentrated in chapters 8–10.

NOTE ON TRANSLATIONS AND ABBREVIATIONS OF RABBINIC SOURCES

Where possible, the parables have been taken from standard English translations, but we have sometimes modified them when a more literal rendering of the Hebrew would result in greater uniformity. Thus we have attempted to provide consistent and literal translations of the formulae that introduce parables and those that indicate the transition from parable to interpretation. Also we have on occasion provided a literal translation of a Hebrew idiom—for example, when God is referred to as "the Place." For some works English translations did not exist, and we have made our own translation from the Hebrew, referring when possible to German or French versions. For the rabbinic documents in their original texts and for modern translations, see the excellent bibliography provided by John T. Townsend, "Rabbinic Sources," in *The Study of Judaism* (New York: Ktav, 1972), pp. 35–80.

Our selection of rabbinic parables is drawn from fourteen sources. We here describe the situation as to translations and abbreviations used in referring to them. The order here follows that in which the sources will appear in part 1.

The Mishnah

We use the translation by Herbert Danby (London: Oxford University Press, 1967). Since this work is divided into sixty-three tractates, each with a Hebrew or Aramaic name, references are given by the name of the tractate preceded by "M.," together with the chapter and section numbers; thus: M. Aboth 3:18.

Tosefta

Because at the time we did our work no suitable translation of Tosefta existed, we made our own. Recently a complete English translation under the leadership of Jacob Neusner has appeared (New York: Ktav, 1977–1986). This source is divided into fifty-nine tractates with names identical to corresponding tractates in the Mishnah. "Tos." precedes the name of the tractate plus chapter and section; thus: Tos. Sotah 7:11.

Palestinian Talmud

This work is popularly called the Jerusalem Talmud. There is as yet no complete English translation, though one is now being prepared under the direction of Jacob Neusner. There is a faulty French translation by Moïse Schwab, originally published in eleven volumes (Paris, 1871–90) and reprinted in six volumes (Paris: Maisonneuve, 1961). Both this Talmud and the next item are expansions made upon the Mishnah. Reference to the Palestinian Talmud is by name of the tractate preceded by "P.," together with the chapter and section number of Mishnah that the Talmud is expanding upon; thus: P. Hagigah 2:1.

Babylonian Talmud

An English translation in eighteen volumes has appeared under the editorship of Isidore Epstein (London: Soncino, 1948–52). In references "B" precedes the tractate, followed by folio number and side ("a" or "b"); thus: B. Shabbath 163a.

Aboth de Rabbi Nathan

There are two recensions of this source. Recension A has two translations: by Judah Goldin, *The Fathers According to Rabbi Nathan*, Yale Judaica Series, 10 (New Haven: Yale University Press, 1955); and by Eli Cashdan, volume 1 of *The Minor Tractates of the Talmud*, edited under the editorship of the Rev. Dr. A. Cohen (London: Soncino, 1956). Recension B has been translated by Anthony J. Saldarini, *The Fathers According to Rabbi Nathan (Abot de Rabbi Nathan), Version B*, Studies in Judaism in Late Antiquity, 11 (Leiden: E. J. Brill, 1975). References to this work include recension; thus: ARNa 1:8 or ARNb 1.

Other Minor Tractates of the Talmud

A translation in two volumes has been prepared under the leadership of A. Cohen (London: Soncino Press, 1965; 2d ed., 1971). References give the full name of the individual tractate; thus: Soferim 16:2.

Mekilta de Rabbi Ishmael

An excellent text and translation is provided by Jacob Z. Lauterbach in three volumes (Philadelphia: Jewish Publication Society, 1933–35). References are given as "Mek." plus the name of the tractate and chapter and line number(s);

thus: Mek. Shirata 3:78. As in all the translations, we have made some modifications in the interest of greater uniformity with our other translations and literalness. At the request of the publisher we indicate by footnote where this is done.

Sifra on Leviticus

There is no complete English translation (though one is now in process of publication under the editorship of Jacob Neusner), but a German translation was prepared by Jakob Winter, *Sifra: Halachischer Midrasch zu Leviticus*, Schriften der Gesellschaft des Judentums, 24 (Breslau: Stefan Munz, 1938). Reference is to chapter and verse in Leviticus upon which this midrash is commenting; thus: Sifra on Leviticus 8:15.

Sifre on Numbers

There is no complete English translation, but see the German translation by K. G. Winter, *Der tannaitische Midrasch Sifre zu Numeri*, Rabbinische Texte, 2d ser.: Tannaitische Midraschim, 3 (Stuttgart: W. Kohlhammer, 1959). Selections are translated into English by Levertoff, which we have used. References are given by section number in this midrash; thus: Sifre on Numbers 82.

Sifre on Deuteronomy

See the German translation by Henrik Ljungman, *Sifre zu Deuteronomium*, Rabbinische Texte, 2d ser.: Tannaitische Midraschim, 4 (Stuttgart: W. Kohlhammer, 1964). Reference is to section number in the Finkelstein-Horovitz edition of the Hebrew text; thus: Sifre on Deuteronomy 8. There are now two English translations: Reuven Hammer, *Sifre: A Tannaitic Commentary on the Book of Deuteronomy* (New Haven: Yale University Press, 1986); and Jacob Neusner, *Sifre to Deuteronomy: An Analytical Translation* (Atlanta: Scholars, 1987). We have generally retained our own translations.

Midrash Rabbah Series

Midrashic commentaries on Genesis, Leviticus, Deuteronomy, and the Song of Songs are parts of the ten-part series of midrashim known as the Midrash Rabbah (Great commentary), which was translated under the editorship of H. Freedman and Maurice Simon (London: Soncino, 1939; compact edition in five volumes, 1977). References are given with the abbreviated name of the canonical book followed by "R.," together with the chapter and section of the commentary; thus: Song R. 3:7:1.

Other Abbreviations

Two other abbreviations that appear frequently in the following pages as part of personal names are "R." for "Rabbi," and "b." for "ben" or "bar," meaning "son of" in Hebrew and Aramaic, respectively. We have not attempted to be consistent in the form of Hebrew and Aramaic names and terms, using traditional English spellings in instances where they are more familiar than strictly consistent transliterations.

Part 1

THE PARABLES

THE PARABLES

Presented here is a selection of 115 parables from the classical rabbinic literature that are ascribed to Tannaim—rabbinic authorities who taught before 220 C.E., the period corresponding to the time of Jesus, the apostles, and the earlier church fathers. The parables are arranged under the various rabbinic works from which they are taken and numbered in sequence so that they can be referred to easily in the chapters of part 2. An appendix of ten irregular items concludes part 1.

Each rabbinic work used is briefly introduced. The works cited here fall generally into two categories: (1) the Mishnah and later works that grew out of it—Tosefta, Palestinian and Babylonian Talmuds, Aboth de Rabbi Nathan, and the so-called Minor Tractates of the Talmud; and (2) the Midrashim—roughly speaking, homiletic or practical commentaries on Scripture. The midrashim that will be cited can be divided by chronology into Tannaitic midrashim (so called because all the authorities cited in them are teachers who antedated 220 C.E.)—Mekilta, Sifra, and Sifre—and the midrashim that compose that collection known as the Midrash Rabbah. We take up the rabbinic works in the order suggested by these classifications.

The original language of these parables was Hebrew.

When we use an existing English translation (see Introduction), we sometimes take the liberty of modifying it where necessary in the interests of uniformity.

For each parable we supply the following information in the headings: title, teacher to whom ascribed, approximate date, location within the work, and, as appropriate, the location elsewhere in rabbinic literature of doublets or close parallels, especially when ascribed to Tannaim. The parables proper are generally preceded by the illustrand (the point that the parable is intended to prove or illustrate) or other introductory comment and are followed by the concluding apodosis, application, or interpretation. Biblical quotations are set off by quotation marks, followed by chapter-and-verse reference.

Brackets indicate words supplied to clarify the meaning when a more literal translation would be too ambiguous, to enclose summaries of illustrands when they are too long to be quoted verbatim, and to set off brief notes that we have appended to many of the items. Where two or three successive parables compose a single pericope in the source (e.g., nos. 3–4), they are considered together.

THE MISHNAH

According to rabbinic tradition, the Mishnah was compiled by R. Judah ha-Nasi between 200 and 220 C.E. It contains traditions from earlier generations that were passed down orally from teacher to disciple before being at last written down and codified. Arranged topically into sixty-three tractates, it is, after the Bible, the fundamental document of Jewish law. Because the work is mostly a no-nonsense code of laws, there are few parables in it. A few parable-like items can be gleaned from it, however, especially from the tractate known as Pirqe Aboth (Chapters of the Fathers). Out of ten such items we here present four.

1. *The Ill-Treated Cupbearer; anonymous; before 220;*
   M. Sukkah 2:9

Throughout the seven days [of the feast] a man must make his *sukkah* [booth] a regular abode and his house a chance abode. If rain fell, when may he vacate [the *sukkah*]? When a dish of porridge would spoil.

They parable a parable. Unto what is the matter like? It is like a slave who came to fill the cup for his master, and he [the master] poured the pitcher over his [the slave's] face.

[During the Feast of Tabernacles (see Lev. 23:34–36), Jews were commanded to dwell in temporary shelters for seven days. By taking their meals in these booths, they made them their primary abode. If it rained during the feast, it was considered a sign of a curse (M. Taanith 1:1), of God's anger. The parable is saying that if it rains when Israel does its duty of observing the festival, it is like a master becoming angry at his slave for doing his duty.]

2. *The Well-Rooted Tree; R. Eleazar b. Azariah; ca. 90; M. Aboth 3:18 (cf. ARNa 22:2; ARNb 34)*

He whose wisdom is more abundant than his works, unto what is he like? He is like a tree whose branches are abundant but whose roots are few. And the wind comes and uproots it and overturns it.

As it is written: "He shall be like a tamarisk in the desert and shall not see when good cometh: but shall inhabit the parched places in the wilderness" (Jer. 17:6).

But he whose works are more abundant than his wisdom, unto what is he like? He is like a tree whose branches are few but whose roots are many; so that even if all the winds in the world come and blow against it, it cannot be stirred from its place.

As it is written: "He shall be as a tree planted by the waters, and that spreadeth out his roots by the river, and shall not fear when heat cometh, and his leaf shall be green: and shall not be careful in the year of drought, neither shall cease from yielding fruit" (Jer. 17:8).

[Some manuscripts and texts omit the proof texts quoted from Jeremiah, which makes the resemblance to Matt. 7:24–27 much greater.]

3–4. *The Ink on New Paper, The Eater of Ripe Grapes;*
Elisha b. Abuyah, ca. 120; R. Jose b. Judah of Kefar
ha-Babli, ca. 190; M. Aboth 4:20 (cf. ARNa 23:3;
ARNb 35)

[3] Elisha b. Abuyah said: He that learns as a child, unto what is he like? He is like ink written on new paper. He that learns as an old man, unto what is he like? He is like ink written on paper that has been blotted out.

[4] R. Jose b. Judah of Kefar ha-Babli said: He that learns from the young, unto what is he like? He is like one that eats unripe grapes and drinks wine from his winepress. And he that learns from the aged, unto what is he like? He is like one that eats ripe grapes and drinks old wine.

Rabbi said: Look not on the jar but on what is in it: there may be a new jar that is full of old wine and an old one in which is not even new wine.

TOSEFTA

Tosefta, which was probably edited about 400 C.E., is a supplement to the Mishnah. The authorities cited in it are Tannaitic, and it is topically organized into tractates with the same titles as the corresponding Mishnah tractates, although four of the Mishnaic tractates have no counterpart in Tosefta. Though Tosefta lacks a tractate corresponding to Aboth, it contains more parables than does the Mishnah. Out of some twenty-four parables or quasi parables in Tosefta, we have selected eleven.

5. *The Inept Servant; anonymous; Tos. Berakoth 7:18*

[Gentiles, women, and uneducated persons cannot be expected to understand the Law.]

They parable a parable. Unto what is the matter like? It is like a king of flesh and blood who told his servant to boil him some broth, though he had never boiled him broth in his life. The result was that he burnt the broth and provoked his master. (He told him) to make him a fold in his shirt, though he had never made him a fold to a shirt in his life. The result was that he soiled the shirt and provoked his master.

6. *The Lamp Removed; anonymous; Tos. Sukkah 2:6 (cf. B. Sukkah 29a)*

When the luminaries are eclipsed, it is an ill omen to the whole world.

Unto what is the matter like? It is like a king who made a banquet and summoned guests. He became angry with them and bade the steward remove the lamp from before them, so that they were all sitting in darkness.

7. *The Street Between Fire and Snow; anonymous; Tos. Hagigah 2:6[5] (cf. ARNa 28:10)*

[This continues a cosmological discussion.] Another interpretation.

They parable a parable. Unto what is the matter like? It is like a street that passes between two paths, one of fire and the other of snow. If one deviates this way, he will be burned by the fire; if he deviates that way, he will be frostbitten. It is profitable for a man to walk in the middle and not be deviating this way or that way.

[The parallel in ARNa occurs in a clearly paraenetic context. It is there attributed to R. Judah b. Ilai, ca. 150.]

8. *The Unfortunate Fugitive; anonymous; Tos. Sotah 15:7*

When the Sanhedrin was abolished, song was abolished from the wedding banquets [lit., "house of drinking"]. And for what was the Sanhedrin profitable to Israel? It was as their eyes, as it is written: "And if the people of the land do at all hide their eyes from that man" (Lev. 20:4). After the Sanhedrin was established, they [malefactors] were destroyed from Israel, but now [that there is no Sanhedrin], they are destroyed from Israel and their families are punished, as it is written: "Then I will set My face against that man and against his family" (v. 5).

A parable. It is like one who committed an offense in the city. They delivered him to a murderer, and he barely escaped from the murderer. They delivered him to the governor, and he barely escaped from the governor. They delivered him to the rod-bearers, and they threw him into a furnace.

Even so, the latter troubles cause the first to be forgotten.

[The text is corrupt, and the manuscripts exhibit many variants. Cf. the translation of Jacob Neusner.]

9–11. The Protected Vineyard and Vine, The Married Woman, The Fenced Vineyard; Rabban Gamaliel; ca. 80; Tos. Kiddushin 1:11

R. Judah [b. Ilai] says: Everyone who does not teach his son a handicraft, teaches him thievery.

[9] R. Gamaliel says: Everyone who has a handicraft, unto what is he like? He is like a vineyard that is surrounded by a fence, and like a vine tendril surrounded by an enclosure.

[10] R. Jose says in the name of Rabban Gamaliel: Everyone who has a handicraft, unto what is he like? He is like a woman who has a husband. Whether she adorns herself or not, no one gets fresh with her. If she does adorn herself, she will have no fear [a textual variant: "If she does not adorn herself, there will be a curse upon her"]. Everyone who has not a handicraft, unto what is he like? He is like a woman who has no husband. Whether she adorns herself or not, everyone is fresh with her. And even when she does not adorn herself, she has fear [textual variants corresponding to the previous one].

[11] R. Eleazar b. Zadok said in the name of Rabban Gamaliel: Everyone who has a handicraft, unto what is he like? He is like an enclosed vineyard into which neither cattle nor wild beasts trespass, and the passers-by do not eat what is in it and do not see what is in it. And everyone who has no handicraft, unto what is he like? He is like an unfenced vineyard, into which cattle and wild beasts trespass, and the passers-by eat what is in it and see what is in it.

12. *The Two Men Who Slighted Royalty; Rabban Gamaliel;
ca. 80; Tos. Baba Kamma 7:2 (cf. B. Baba Kamma 79b)*

[Isa. 29:15; Ps. 34:7; and Ezek. 8:12 quoted.]

R. Meir said: They parable a parable in the name of
Rabban Gamaliel. Unto what is the matter like? It is like two
men who planned a great wedding feast in the city. One
invited the inhabitants of the city but did not invite the king.
The other invited neither the king nor the inhabitants of the
city. Whose punishment will be the greater? That of the one
who invited the inhabitants of the city but not the king.

[The parallel occurs in the context of an answer to the
question of why the Torah was more severe on a thief than
on a robber.]

13. *The Wife Sent Back to Her Father; R. Johanan b. Zakkai;
ca. 70; Tos. Baba Kamma 7:3. (cf. B. Pesahim 87b)*

Five things were said by R. Johanan b. Zakkai in the
nature of a principle. Why did Israel go into exile into
Babylon rather than into all other lands? Because the home of
Abraham was from there.

They parable a parable. Unto what is the matter like? It
is like a woman who disgraces her husband so that he sends
her away. He sends her away to the home of her father.

[In the parallel the wife is sent to "the home of her
mother."]

14. *The Wife's Documents; Johanan b. Zakkai; ca. 70; Tos.
Baba Kamma 7:4 (cf. Deut. R. 3:17; Exod. R. 47:2)*

In the case of the first tablets [of the Decalogue]: "And
the tables were the work of God" (Exod. 32:16). In the case of
the second set of tablets, the tables were the work of Moses,
as it is written: "And he [Moses] wrote upon the tablets the
words of the covenant, the Decalogue" (Exod. 34:28).

They parable a parable. Unto what is the matter like? It
is like a king of flesh and blood who became engaged to a
woman. He brought the scribe and ink and pen and the

document and the witnesses. But if the woman had been divorcing him, she would bring all the necessary items. It would be enough for it that the king provided his own signature for the document.

[The Deuteronomy R. version, which is much later, is both clearer and more elaborate. The parable depends on the ancient customs of drawing up a marriage contract and of giving a bill of divorcement (cf. Deut. 24:1).]

15. *The King's Twin Who Was Executed; R. Meir; ca. 140; Tos. Sanhedrin 9:7 (cf. B. Sanhedrin 46b)*

R. Meir says: What does the Scripture mean: "For that which is hanged is a curse of God" (Deut. 21:23)?

It is like two twin brothers, each resembling the other. One became king over the whole world, and the other went out into robbery. After a time the one who went out into robbery was captured and they crucified (hanged) him on a cross (gallows). And all the passers-by were saying: It is as though the king were crucified.

Therefore it is said: "For that which is hanged is a curse of God."

["Curse of God" is understood here to mean that God is the object of the curse. The parable hinges on the fact that man was created in God's image, and he is thus in a sense God's "twin." The parallel adds the details that the king commanded the robber to be hanged and commanded him to be taken down.]

PALESTINIAN TALMUD

The compilation and redaction of the Palestinian Talmud was never really completed, but it ended about 400 C.E. Its popular designation *Yerushalmi* (Jerusalem Talmud) cannot be technically correct, since after the destruction of the temple there was no more academy in Jerusalem; the schools that produced this Talmud were at Tiberias, Sepphoris, and Caesarea. We have found some thirty parabolic items in this source, only about five of them possibly Tannaitic. We present here one of them.

16. The Brazen and Proper Daughters; R. Akiba; ca. 95; P. Taanith 3:4

R. Eliezer observed a fast but caused no rain to fall. R. Akiba observed a fast, and rain fell.

He (R. Akiba) went in and spoke before them, saying: I will parable to you a parable. Unto what is the matter like? It is like a king who had two daughters. One was brazen, and one was proper. Whenever the brazen one wanted something and went in before him, he said: Give her what she wants so she will get out of here. But whenever the proper one wanted something and went in before him, he prolonged the conversation with her because her speaking so pleased him.

But is it permissible to disparage oneself in public? Only to glorify the divine name, that it be not supposed that some lack in R. Eliezer may have prevented his success.

[Parables 22–23 are partially parallel. This item is followed by an anecdote about a much later Rabbi who observed thirteen fasts without rain falling.]

BABYLONIAN TALMUD

The compilation and redaction of the Babylonian Talmud at the rabbinic academies of Mesopotamia was probably completed around 550 C.E. Like the Palestinian Talmud, it contains numerous *baraitoth* (sayings of the Tannaim that were not included in the Mishnah). Out of some thirty-six items that we considered to be attributed to Tannaim, we here present nine.

17. The Man with a Fine Beard; R. Eleazar b. Azariah; ca. 80; B. Berakoth 11a

Once R. Ishmael and R. Eleazar b. Azariah were dining at the same place, and R. Ishmael was reclining while R. Eleazar was standing upright. When the time came for reciting the Shema, R. Eleazar reclined, and R. Ishmael stood upright. Said R. Eleazar b. Azariah to R. Ishmael:

Brother Ishmael, I will parable you a parable. Unto what

is the matter like? A parable. It is like one to whom people say: You have a fine beard. And he says: Let this go to meet the destroyers. [By these words the man rejects the compliment.]

So with you. As long as I was upright, you were reclining, and now that I recline, you stand upright! He replied: I have acted according to the rule of Beth Hillel, and you have acted according to the rule of Beth Shammai. And what is more (I had to act thus), lest the disciples should see and fix the halakah so for future generations!

[The Shema (Hear!) is the words of Deut. 6:4–9, which, along with certain other texts, Jewish men recited every morning and evening. *Halakah* is a term referring to rabbinic law, the rules of Jewish living. Beth (house of) Hillel and Beth Shammai were two rival schools of legal interpretation within Pharisaism and rabbinic Judaism. R. Ishmael's parable implied that R. Eleazar had refused to follow his example just to spite him. But R. Eleazar explained that he did the opposite of what R. Ishmael did to teach their followers that in these particular matters *either* reclining or standing was proper.]

18. *The Fox and the Fishes; R. Akiba; ca. 135; B. Berakoth 61b*

Our Rabbis taught: Once the wicked Government [i.e., the Romans] issued a decree forbidding the Jews to study and practice the Torah. Pappus b. Judah came and found R. Akiba publicly bringing gatherings together and occupying himself with the Torah. He said to him: Akiba, are you not afraid of the government?

He said to him: I will parable to thee a parable. Unto what is the matter like? It is like a fox who was walking alongside a river, and he saw fishes going in swarms from one place to another. He said to them: From what are you fleeing? They replied: From the nets cast for us by men. He said to them: Would you like to come onto the dry land so that you and I can live together in the way that my ancestors lived with your ancestors? They said to him: Art thou the one that they call the cleverest of the animals? Thou art not clever but foolish. If we are afraid in the element in which we live, how much more in the element in which we would die!

So it is with us. If such is our condition when we sit and study the Torah, of which it is written, "For that is thy life and the length of thy days" (Deut. 30:20), if we go and neglect it, how much worse off we shall be.

[Here Akiba turns to rabbinic purposes an old fable mediated to him through Hellenistic sources. It came originally from India, where it can be found in *Baka Jataka*, a collection of Buddhist legends.]

19. *The Wise and Foolish Invitees; R. Johanan b. Zakkai; ca. 70; B. Shabbath 153a (cf. Eccl. R. 9:8:1)*

We learned elsewhere, R. Eliezer said: Repent one day before your death [cf. Sirach 5:7]. His disciples asked him: Does one know on what day he will die? He said: Then all the more reason that he repent today, lest he die tomorrow, and thus his whole life is spent in repentance. And Solomon too said in his wisdom: "Let thy garments be always white; and let not thy head lack ointment" (Eccl. 9:8).

R. Johanan b. Zakkai said: A parable. It is like a king who summoned his servants to a banquet without appointing a time. The wise ones adorned themselves and sat at the door of the palace; they said: Is anything lacking in a royal palace? The fools went about their work, saying: Can there be a banquet without preparations? Suddenly the king desired the presence of his servants. The wise entered adorned, while the fools entered soiled. The king rejoiced at the wise but was angry with the fools. He said: Those who adorned themselves for the banquet, let them sit, eat, and drink. But those who did not adorn themselves for the banquet, let them stand and watch.

R. Meir's son-in-law said in R. Meir's name: Then they too would merely look on, being in attendance. But both sit, the former eating and the latter hungering, the former drinking and the latter thirsting, for it is said: "Therefore thus saith the Lord God: Behold, My servants shall eat, but ye shall be hungry; behold, My servants shall drink, but ye shall be thirsty; behold My servants shall rejoice, but ye shall be ashamed; behold, My servants shall sing for joy of heart, but ye shall cry for sorrow of heart" (Isa. 65:13–14).

[The parallel attributes the parable to R. Judah ha-Nasi.]

20. *The King Who Did Not Exempt Himself from Taxes; R. Simeon b. Yohai; ca. 140; B. Sukkah 30a*

R. Johanan in the name of R. Simeon b. Yohai further said: What is the purport of that which is written: "For I the Lord love justice, I hate robbery with iniquity" (Isa. 61:8)?

It is like a king of flesh and blood who passed through his customhouse and said to his attendants: Pay the tax to the tax collectors. They said to him: But the whole tax, surely, belongs to thee. He said to them: All travelers would learn from me not to evade their payments of tax.

So the Holy One, blessed be He, said: "I the Lord hate robbery in burnt offerings" [the term may mean either "iniquity" or "burnt offerings"]; let my children learn from me and keep away from robbery.

21. *The Borrower Who Defaulted; R. Jose the Priest; ca. 90; B. Rosh ha-Shanah 17b–18a*

Bluria the Proselyte put this question to Rabban Gamaliel: It is written in your Law: "Who lifteth not up the countenance" (Deut. 10:17), and it is also written: "The Lord shall lift up His countenance upon thee" (Num. 6:26).

R. Jose the Priest joined the conversation and said to her: I will parable to thee a parable. Unto what is the matter like? It is like one who lent his neighbor a *maneh* and fixed a time for payment in the presence of the king, while the other swore to pay him by the life of the king. When the time arrived, he did not pay him, and he went to excuse himself to the king. But the king said to him: The wrong done to me, I excuse you, but go and obtain forgiveness from your neighbor.

Even so, one text speaks of offenses committed by a man against God,* the other of offenses committed by a man

---

*Here and elsewhere in rabbinic writings (but not in Scripture), the Hebrew uses a circumlocution for God—in this case, "the Place."

against his fellow man. (This explanation was generally accepted) until R. Akiba came and taught: One text speaks of God's attitude before the final sentence, the other of his attitude after the final sentence! Here too the case is that of an individual.

[A *maneh* (Hebrew), or *mina* (Greek), was worth 100 dinars, or denarii—a substantial sum of money; one denarius was the normal wage of an agricultural laborer for one day's work (cf. Matt. 20:2).]

22–23. The Master Who Gave Promptly, The Master Who Gave Slowly; R. Samuel the Younger; ca. 90; B. Taanith 25b

[22] Samuel the Younger ordained a fast, and rain fell before sunrise. The people thought it was due to the merit of the community, whereupon he said to them:

I will parable to you a parable. Unto what is the matter like? It is like a servant who asked his master for a gratuity, and the master said: Give it to him, and let me not hear his voice.

[23] Another time Samuel the Younger ordained a fast, and rain fell after sunset. The people thought that it was due to the merit of the community, whereupon Samuel said:

I will parable to you a parable. Unto what is the matter like? It is like a servant who asked his master for a gratuity, and the master said: Keep him waiting until he is made submissive and is distressed, and then give him his gratuity.

According to Samuel the Younger, what would be an instance of rain falling on account of the merit of the community? If they recited [the prayer] "He Causeth the Rain to Fall," and rain fell.

24. The Trees with Overhanging Boughs; R. Eleazar b. Zadok; ca. 90; B. Kiddushin 40b (cf. ARNa 39:1)

R. Eleazar son of R. Zadok said: Unto what are the righteous compared [*nimshelim*] in this world? They are like a tree standing wholly in a place of cleanness, but its bough overhangs a place of uncleanness. When the bough is lopped off, it stands entirely in a place of cleanness.

Even so the Holy One, blessed be He, brings suffering upon the righteous in this world in order that they may inherit the future world, as it is said: "And though thy beginning is small, yet thy latter end shall greatly increase" (Job 8:7).

And unto what are the wicked compared in this world? They are like a tree standing wholly in a place of uncleanness, but a branch thereof overhangs a place of cleanness. When the bough is lopped off, it stands entirely in a place of uncleanness.

25. *The Aborted Wedding Celebration; R. Joshua b. Karha; ca. 150; B. Sanhedrin 108a (cf. Gen. R. 28:6)*

"And every living substance was destroyed which was upon the face of the ground (both man and cattle)" (Gen. 7:23). If man sinned, how did the beasts sin?

A Tanna taught in the name of R. Joshua b. Karha: A parable. It is like a man who made a bridal chamber for his son, and he prepared a banquet with every variety of food. Subsequently his son died, whereupon he arose and broke up the feast and said: Have I prepared all this for any but my son? Now that he is dead, what need have I of the banquet?

Also [*aph*] the Holy One, blessed be He, said: Did I create the animals and beasts for aught but man? Now that man has sinned, what need have I of the animals and beasts?

ABOTH DE RABBI NATHAN

The "Fathers of Rabbi Nathan" is the longest of the so-called Minor Tractates appended to the fourth division of the Babylonian Talmud. It is a sort of commentary upon a version of the Mishnah tractate Pirqe Aboth (or simply "Aboth") earlier than the one we now have in the Mishnah. It survives in two recensions: *A*, cited by Ashkenazi (northern European) Rabbis; and *B*, cited by Sephardi (Mediterranean) Rabbis. It is best dated in the third or fourth century, though it perhaps existed in some form even earlier than the final editing of the Mishnah, about 220 C.E. The authorities cited in this work are all Tannaim, except in a very few glosses. Out of some sixteen parables in Recension A, we here present ten.

26. *The Bad Example; R. Simeon b. Eleazar; ca. 170; ARNa 1:8 (cf. ARNb 1, Schechter ed., pp. 6–7)*

[Discussion of the fall of Adam.]

R. Simeon b. Eleazar says: I will parable to thee a parable. Unto what is the matter like? It is like a certain man who married a proselyte. He used to sit admonishing her. He said: My dear, do not eat bread when thy hands are defiled, do not eat untithed produce, do not profane the Sabbath, do not make vows rashly, and do not go about with another man. If thou transgress any of these, thou shalt surely die. Now, what did that man do [textual uncertainty]? He arose and ate in her presence bread although his hands were defiled, he ate before her untithed produce, he profaned the Sabbath, he made vows rashly, and he brought out to her [textual uncertainty]. What did that proselyte say in her heart? All the things about which my husband admonished me in the beginning are false. Forthwith she arose and transgressed them all.

[While this version of the parable blames the man, the parallel in Recension B puts the blame on the woman. Probably the version in Recension A is original. Both the places of textual confusion and the version in Recension B resulted from an attempt to assimilate R. Simeon's parable better to the context for which it is adduced.]

27. *The Curious Wife and the Scorpion; R. Simeon b. Yohai; ca. 140; ARNa 1:8 (cf. ARNb 1, Schechter ed., pp. 7–8; Gen. R. 19:10; Pirqe de R. Eliezer 13)*

[Follows the preceding parable.]

R. Simeon b. Yohai says: I will parable to thee a parable. Unto what is the matter like? [variant reading: "Unto what is the first man like?"] It is like one who had a wife at home. What did the man do? He went and brought a jar and put into it figs and nuts, a definite number of them. And he caught a scorpion and put it in the mouth of the jar, and he sealed the jar with a tight-fitting lid and put it in a corner. He said to her [his wife]: My dear [lit., "my daughter"], everything I have in this house is in thy hands, except this jar, which thou mayest not touch at all. What did the woman do? As soon as her husband went out to the marketplace, she arose and opened the jar and stuck her hand into it, and the scorpion stung her. She went and fell upon her bed. When her husband returned from the marketplace, he said to her: What is this? She said to him: My hand I put in the jar, and a scorpion stung me, and now I am dying! He said to her: Did I not tell thee so in the beginning that everything I have in the house is in thy hands, except this jar, which thou mayest not touch at all? He straightway became angry with her, and he drove her out.

Even so was Adam [or, "the first man"], when the Holy One, blessed be He, said to him: "Of every tree of the garden thou mayest freely eat; but of the tree of the knowledge of good and evil, thou shalt not eat of it: for in the day thou eatest thereof, thou shalt surely die" (Gen. 2:16–17). As soon as Adam ate of it, he was driven out, to fulfill that which is said: "Man tarrieth not overnight in his glory; he is like the beasts that perish" (Ps. 49:12 [MT v. 13]).

[This parable seems to owe much to the Greek story of Pandora and the Box (Hesiod, *Theogony*, 570–93; *Works and Days*, 80–105, but it has been partially adapted to its new context as an illustration of the story of Adam's fall in Genesis. The parallel in Recension B carries this adaptation further; this parallel is repeated in Gen. R. 19:10 and Pirqe de R. Eliezer 13.]

28. *The Retracted Betrothal; R. Jose the Galilean; ca. 130; ARNa 2:3 (cf. ARNb 2, Schechter ed., p. 10; Exod. R. 43:1; Pesikta Rabbati 20:2)*

[Discussion of why Moses broke the tablets of the law when he found Israel worshiping the golden calf.]

R. Jose the Galilean says: I will parable to thee a parable. Unto what is the matter like? It is like a king of flesh and blood who said to his agent: Go and betroth for me a beautiful, amiable, and well-behaved maiden. The agent went and performed the betrothal. After the betrothal, he went and discovered that she played the harlot with another. Straightway on his own authority he made a decision. He said: If I now give her the contract, she will be liable to the death penalty, and she will be taken away from my master for ever.

Even so was Moses. On his own authority he made a decision. He said: How shall I give these tablets to Israel? It will make them accountable for the major commandments and thus make them liable to the death penalty, for it is written in the tablets: "He that sacrificeth unto the gods, save unto the Lord only, shall be utterly destroyed" (Exod. 22:20 [MT v. 19]). I will rather seize the tablets and break them and lead Israel back to the right way. Then Israel might say: Where are the first tablets that you brought down? There were no such things at all!

[The parallel versions in Recension B and Exodus Rabbah fill out the details to make the story more complete. The story is transformed but still recognizable in Pesikta Rabbati 20. The parable hangs on ancient marriage customs. Marriages were usually arranged, and betrothals could be performed by proxy. A marriage contract was always drawn up.]

29. *The Persistent Stonecutter; R. Simeon b. Eleazar; ca. 170; ARNa 6:2 (cf. ARNb 12, Schechter ed., p. 29)*

[Account of R. Akiba's perseverance in learning.]
R. Simeon b. Eleazar says: I will parable to thee a parable. Unto what is the matter like? It is like a stonecutter who was hacking away in the mountains. Once he took his pickax in his hand and went and sat on the mountain and was chipping away from it small stones. And some men came and said to him: What art thou doing? He said to them: Behold, I am uprooting it and casting it into the Jordan. They said to him: Thou canst not uproot the whole mountain! He kept on hacking away until it became the size of a large boulder. He crawled under it, loosened it and uprooted it, and cast it into the Jordan. And he said to it: This is not thy place, but there!

Even so did R. Akiba with (the instruction of) R. Eliezer and R. Joshua.

[The parallel version is attributed to Simeon b. Menasiah.]

30. *The Man of One Field; R. Meir; ca. 150; ARNa 8:2 (cf. ARNb 18, Schechter ed., p. 39)*

[Commenting on the saying in M. Aboth 1:6, "Provide thyself with a teacher."]

R. Meir used to say: He that learns Torah from one teacher, unto what is he like? He is like one who had a single field, and he sowed it partly with wheat and partly with barley and planted part with olives and part with fruit trees. And it happens that that man is full of good and blessings. But when one learns from two or three teachers, he is like one who has many fields. One he sows with wheat, and one he sows with barley; and he plants one with olives and one with fruit trees. And it happens that that man's (attention) is divided among many pieces of land, without good or blessing.

31. *The Depositary for the King; R. Eleazar b. Arak; ca. 90; ARNa 14:6*

[When the son of R. Johanan b. Zakkai died, various Rabbis came and sought to comfort him, but he rejected their words of condolence.] Then R. Eleazar [b. Arak] entered and sat before him and said to him:

I will parable to thee a parable. Unto what is the matter like? It is like a man with whom the king deposited a deposit. Every single day the man would weep and cry out and say: Woe unto me! When shall I be quit of this responsibility in peace?

Also thou, master, hadst a son. He read Torah—the Pentateuch, the Prophets, the Hagiographa; Mishnah, halakoth, and aggadoth. He has departed sinless from this world. And thou shouldst be comforted when thou hast returned thy trust unimpaired.

Said Rabban Johanan to him: Eleazar, my son, thou hast comforted me in the manner men should give comfort.

32. *The False Companion; R. Judah ha-Nasi; ca. 200; ARNa 16:3*

R. Judah ha-Nasi says: I will parable to thee a parable. Unto what is the evil inclination like? It is like two men who enter an inn, and one of them is seized on a charge of robbery. They ask him: Who was with thee? He could say: My companion was not with me. But he says: Since I am to be slain, let my companion be slain along with me.

Also even so says the evil inclination: Since I am doomed in the world to come, I will drag the whole body with me to destruction.

[This is the second in a group of three parables in ARNa dealing with "evil inclination" (*yetzer ha-ra*). Classical rabbinic teaching was that man is created with two natures, or inclinations—an evil one and a good one. The evil one is necessary for existence in this world, for without selfishness and aggressive behavior man would not preserve himself; but this evil nature must be kept in check by obedience to the Torah, and for the righteous, there will be deliverance from it in the world to come.]

33. *The Inferior Field; R. Simeon b. Yohai; ca. 140; ARNa 16:3; ARNb 30*

R. Simeon b. Yohai says: How do we know that Israel will never see the face of Gehenna?

They parable a parable. Unto what is the matter like? It is like a king of flesh and blood who had an inferior field. Some men came and rented it at ten *kor*s of wheat per year. They fertilized it, tilled it, watered it, cleared it, but harvested from it no more than one *kor* of wheat for the year. The king said to them: What is this? They said to him: Our lord, the king! Thou knowest that from the field that thou didst give us, thou didst harvest naught at first. And now that we have fertilized it and cleared it and watered it, we harvested from it at least one *kor* of wheat!

Also even so will Israel plead before the Holy One, blessed be He: Master of the Universe, Thou knowest that the evil impulse stirs us up, as it is said: "For He knoweth our impulse" (Ps. 103:14).

[This is the third in a group of three parables dealing with the evil impulse. See no. 32. Gehenna signifies the place of ultimate punishment. A *kor* was a unit of dry measure, sometimes called a *homer*, equal to about eleven bushels. It is mentioned in Luke 16:7.]

34. *The Palace with a Tannery Pipe; R. Simeon b. Eleazar;*
    ca. 170; ARNa 19:3 (cf. Kallah Rabbati 6 [53b])

[Follows a discussion of Job 25:6, "Surely man is a worm, and the son of man is a maggot."]

R. Simeon b. Eleazar says: I will parable to thee a parable. Unto what is the matter like? It is like a king who built a great palace and adorned it [textual variant: "who built great palaces and dwelt in all of them"], but a tannery pipe led through it and emptied at its doorway. Every passer-by said: How beautiful and magnificent this palace would be if it were not for the tannery pipe coming through it!

Also even so is man thus. If now, with a foul stream issuing from his bowels, he exalts himself over other creatures, how much the more would he exalt himself over other creatures if a stream of precious oil, balsam, or ointment issued from him.

[There is also a partial parallel in Derek Eretz Rabbah 3:2, but there the tannery pipe corresponds also to the mouth.]

35. *The Drawing Space; R. Jose the Galilean; ca. 130; ARNa*
    31:3

R. Jose the Galilean says: All that the Holy One, blessed be He, created in the world, He created also in man.

They parable a parable. Unto what is the matter like? It is like one who takes a wooden tablet and tries to draw many forms. He is hard put to it because he has no room to make the drawings. But he who draws on the earth can go on drawing many forms and spread them out.

But the Holy One, blessed be He—may His great name be blessed forever and to all eternity—in His wisdom and understanding created the whole world, created the heavens and the earth and the beings on high and those down below, and formed in man whatever He created in His world. He created forests in the world, and He created forests in man: namely, man's hair. He created evil beasts in the world, and He created evil beasts in man: namely, the vermin in man. . . .

[The application continues with a long string of analogies between man and the world, of which we have quoted only the first two, establishing that man is a microcosm.]

OTHER MINOR TRACTATES

The Aboth de Rabbi Nathan was only the longest of some fifteen so-called Minor Tractates (*Massektoth Qetannoth*) appended to the fourth division (Nezikin) of the Babylonian Talmud. Parables are to be found in the tractates Soferim, Semachoth, Kallah, Kallah Rabbati, Derek Eretz Rabbah, and Derek Eretz Zuta. We here present only one from Semachoth, which began to be compiled in the first century and reached its present form in the eighth century.

36. *The Wise and Foolish Dinner Guests; R. Meir; ca. 140; Semachoth 8:10*

[The previous pericope had described the slaughter of the Jews, which came within twelve months of R. Akiba's martyrdom.]

R. Meir said: They parable a parable. Unto what is the matter like? It is like a king who made a banquet and invited guests without fixing a time when they should leave. The shrewd among them left at the ninth hour [3 P.M.], returned home, and went to bed while it was still light. Others left at sunset while the shops were still open and the lamps burning, entered their homes, and went to bed by the light of the lamps. Still others left at two or three hours in the night when some shops were open and some shut, some with their lights alight and some with their lamps extinguished, entered their homes and went to bed in the dark. Those remaining at the banquet became intoxicated and wounded and killed each other; as it is said: "I saw the Lord standing by the altar; and He said: Smite the capitals, that the posts may shake; and break them in pieces on the head of all of them; and I will slay the residue of them with the sword" (Amos 9:1).

[Perhaps the meaning is that those Jews who came late in the historical scheme had to suffer in the Hadrianic tribulation, while those who left the scene earlier died in peace. R. Akiba passed away in time not to witness the slaughter.]

MEKILTA

Mekilta de Rabbi Ishmael is a midrash on the legal portions of Exodus. There is also a somewhat fragmentary Mekilta de Simeon b. Yohai, which is apparently largely dependent upon the former Mekilta. *Mekilta* without further qualification refers to that of Rabbi Ishmael. This source is counted among the so-called halakic or Tannaitic midrashim, and while it reflects second-century rabbinic law, it is generally held that it was compiled and redacted in Palestine around the end of the fourth century. The authorities cited in it are all Tannaim.

Out of thirty-two parabolic items that we have extracted from Mekilta, we present here twenty-seven.*

37. *The Fugitive Slave in the Cemetery; anonymous; Mek. Pischa 1:80–88*

But Jonah thought: I will go outside of the land, where the Shekinah does not reveal itself. For since the Gentiles are more inclined to repent, I might be causing Israel to be condemned.

---

*As in all our translations, we have made some modifications from that of the original publisher in the interest of greater literalness and uniformity with other translations. In the work cited here, the publisher, the Jewish Publication Society, requests that we indicate in footnotes wherever we have made modification from the original translation of J. Z. Lauterbach.

They parable a parable.[1] It is like a slave who belonged to a priest. He said: I will run away to the cemetery, a place where my master cannot follow me.[2] But his master said to him: I have other heathen slaves like you.

Even so,[3] Jonah said: I will go outside of the land, where the Shekinah[4] does not reveal itself, for since the Gentiles are more inclined to repent, I might be causing Israel to be condemned. But the Holy One, blessed be He, said unto him: I have other agents like you; as it is said: "But the Lord hurled a great wind into the sea" (Jonah 1:4).

[The Shekinah, or divine presence, was one of several common euphemisms for the Deity. Perhaps the most common was "the Holy One, blessed[5] be He." Others were "the Place" and "Heaven." The Law of Moses prohibited priests from having contact with the dead (cf. Lev. 21:11).]

38. *The Proud Father; R. Eleazar b. Azariah; ca. 80; Mek. Pischa 16:62–67*

Then they said to him [R. Joshua]: Master, he [R. Eleazar b. Azariah] also brought out this general idea in the exposition of the text: "Therefore, behold, the days come, saith the Lord, that they shall no more say, As the Lord liveth, that brought up the children of Israel . . . but: As the Lord liveth, that brought up and that led" etc. (Jer. 23:7–8).

They parable a parable.[6] Unto what is the matter like? It is like one who was very desirous of children.[7] After a daughter was born to him, he would swear by the life of the daughter. When again a son was born to him, he left off swearing by the daughter and swore only by the life of the son.

[It is clear from the following parable, with which this

---

[1] Lauterbach: They give a parable for this.
[2] Lauterbach: A priest had a slave who said: "I will run away to the cemetery whither my master cannot follow me."
[3] Lauterbach: Similarly.
[4] Lauterbach: The divine presence.
[5] Lauterbach: Praised.
[6] Lauterbach: One can illustrate it by a parable.
[7] Lauterbach: To what can it be compared? To the following: One was very desirous of children.

one is juxtaposed, that the point is that Israel's second deliverance from captivity overshadows the first.]

39. *The Escape from Three Perils; R. Simeon b. Yohai; ca. 140; Mek. Pischa 16:67–74 (cf. Tos. Berakoth 1:11; B. Berakoth 13a; P. Berakoth 1:9)*

R. Simeon b. Yohai says: They parable a parable.[8] Unto what is the matter like? It is like one who was walking along the road, and he encountered a wolf and was saved from him. And he was going along recounting the story of the wolf. Then he encountered a lion and was saved from him. He forgot the story of the wolf and went along recounting the story of the lion. Then he encountered a serpent and was saved from him. He forgot the story of both of them and went along recounting the story of the serpent.[9]

Even so is Israel.[10] Later troubles cause the former ones to be forgotten.

[This oft-repeated parable has the same point as nos. 8 and 38.]

40. *The Slave and the Rotten Fish; anonymous; Mek. Beshallach 2:107–18 (cf. Pesikta de Rab Kahana 11:3)*

They [the Egyptians] said: If we had been plagued without letting them go, it would have been enough. But we were plagued and let them go. Or if we had been plagued and let them go without our money being taken, it would have been enough. But we were plagued, we let them go, and our money was taken.

A parable. Unto what is the matter like? It is like one

---

[8]Lauterbach: One can illustrate it by a parable.

[9]Lauterbach: To what can it be compared? To the following: One was traveling along the road. He encountered a wolf and was saved from him. So he kept on telling the story of the wolf. Then he encountered a lion and was saved from him. So he forgot the story of the wolf and kept on telling the story of the lion. He then encountered a serpent and was saved from him. So he forgot the story of both of them and kept on telling the story of the serpent.

[10]Lauterbach: So it is with Israel.

who said to his slave:[11] Go get me a fish from the market. The slave went and brought him a bad-smelling[12] fish. He said to the slave: I decree that you eat the fish or receive a hundred lashes or pay a hundred *maneh*. The slave said: I will eat it. He began to eat but could not finish. He therefore said: I will take the lashes. After receiving sixty lashes, he could stand no more. He therefore said: I will pay the hundred *maneh*. The result was that he ate the fish, received lashes, and paid a hundred *maneh*.

So it was done to the Egyptians. They were plagued, they let Israel go, and their money was taken.

[The parallel is attributed to R. Ishmael, ca. 120. For *maneh*, see no. 21.]

41–42. *The Cheaply Sold Field, The Cheaply Sold Estate; R. Jose the Galilean, ca. 120; R. Simeon b. Yohai, ca. 140; Mek. Beshallach 2:142–55 (cf. Pesikta de Rab Kahana 11:7; Song R. 4:12:1; Exod. R. 20:2, 5)*

"And the heart of Pharaoh and his servants was turned" (Exod. 14:5). They said: Has not much good come to us on their account?

[41] R. Jose the Galilean says: A parable. Unto what is the matter like? It is like one to whom there fell as an inheritance a *bet-kor* of land, and he sold it for a trifle.[13] The buyer went and opened up wells in it and planted gardens, trees, and orchards in it. The seller began to choke with regret.

So it happened to the Egyptians who let go without realizing what they let go. Of them it is stated in the tradition:[14] "Thy shoots [or, those whom thou hast sent away] are a park of pomegranates" etc. (Song 4:13).

[42] Another interpretation.

R. Simeon b. Yohai says: A parable. Unto what is the matter like? It is like one to whom there fell as an inheritance

---

[11]Lauterbach: A parable. To what can this be compared? To one who said to his slave:

[12]Lauterbach: Ill-smelling.

[13]Lauterbach: R. Jose the Galilean, giving a parable, says: To what can this be compared? To a man to whom there has fallen as an inheritance a *bet-kor* of land which he sold for a trifle.

[14]Lauterbach: The traditional sacred writings.

a residence in a far-off country, and he sold it for a trifle.[15] The buyer went and discovered in it hidden treasures of silver and of gold, of precious stones and of pearls. The seller began to choke with regret.[16]

So did[17] the Egyptians who let go without realizing what they let go. For it is written: "And they said: What is this we have done that we have let Israel go?" (Exod. 14:5)?

[In some of the versions the sequence of these two parables is reversed. A *bet-kor* of land was presumably enough land to produce a kor of grain (see no. 33).]

43. *The Fleeing Dove; anonymous; Mek. Beshallach 3:86–92 (cf. Song R. 2:14:2)*

[Commenting on the text "Stand still and see the salvation of the Lord" (Exod. 14:13) and discussing the predicament of the Israelites when pursued by the Egyptians.]

Unto what was Israel like at that moment? They were like a dove[18] fleeing from a hawk and about to enter a cleft in the rock where there is a hissing serpent. If she enters, there is the serpent! If she stays out, there is the hawk!

Even so was Israel[19] at that moment, the sea forming a bar and the enemy pursuing. Immediately they set their mind upon prayer. Of them it is stated in the tradition:[20] "O my dove that art in the clefts of the rock" (Song 2:14).

[In the parallel this parable is attributed to the School of Ishmael. A related parable occurs anonymously in Exod. R. 20:6.]

---

[15]Lauterbach: R. Simon the son of Yohai, giving a parable, says: To what can this be compared? To a man to whom there had fallen as an inheritance a residence in a far off country which he sold for a trifle.

[16]Lauterbach: The seller, seeing this, began to choke with grief.

[17]Lauterbach: So also did.

[18]Lauterbach: To what were the Israelites at that moment like? To a dove.

[19]Lauterbach: In such a plight were the Israelites.

[20]Lauterbach: The traditional sacred writings.

44. *The Superfluous Mediator; R. Absalom the Elder; date
unknown but early; Mek. Beshallach 4:35–41 (cf. Exod.
R. 21:8)*

Simon of Teman says: Because of the merit of observing
the commandment of circumcision, I will divide the sea for
them. For it is said: "Thus saith the Lord: If not for My
covenant of day and night, I would not have appointed the
ordinances of heaven and earth" (Jer. 33:25). Go and see
which covenant obtains by day and by night. You can find
none but the covenant of circumcision.

R. Absalom the Elder says: A parable. Unto what is the
matter like? It is like one[21] who got angry with his son and
drove him out of his house. His friend then came to him,
requesting that he allow the son to come back to the house.
He said to his friend: You are only asking me on behalf of my
own son. I am already reconciled to my son.

Even so[22] did the Holy One say to Moses: Wherefore
criest thou? Is it not on behalf of My own sons? I am already
reconciled to My sons. Speak unto the children of Israel that
they go forward.

[In the parallel the parable is cited as a comment on
Exod. 14:15, "Wherefore criest thou unto Me?" which
accords with the application. The parable is there attributed
to "R. Abtulis (or Abtilis) the Elder."]

45. *The Protective Father; R. Judah b. Ilai; ca. 150; Mek.
Beshallach 5:15–31 (cf. Mek. Bachodesh 2:31ff.)*

"And the angel of God . . . removed," etc. (Exod. 14:19).
R. Judah says: Behold, this is a rich verse, echoed in many
places.

A parable. Unto what is the matter like? It is like one
who was walking[23] on the road with his son walking in front
of him. If robbers who might seek to capture the son come

[21]Lauterbach: R. Absolom, the elder, giving a parable, says: To what is
this like? To a man.

[22]Lauterbach: So also did.

[23]Lauterbach: To give a parable, to what is this like? To a man who is
walking.

from in front, he takes him from before himself and puts him behind himself. If a wolf comes from behind, he takes his son from behind and puts him in front. If robbers come from in front and wolves from behind, he takes the son up in his arms. When the son begins to suffer from the sun, his father spreads his cloak over him. When he is hungry, he feeds him; when he is thirsty, he gives him to drink.

So did the Holy One, blessed be He, do, as it is said: "And I, I taught Ephraim to walk, taking them upon My arms: but they knew not that I healed them" (Hos. 11:3). When the son began to suffer from the sun, He spread His cloak over the son, as it is said: "He spread a cloud for a screen" etc. (Ps. 105:39). When he was hungry, He fed him bread, as it is said: "Behold, I will cause to rain bread from heaven for you" (Exod. 16:4). When he was thirsty, He gave him water to drink, as it is said: "He brought streams also out of the rock" (Ps. 78:16). And "streams" here means only living waters, as it is said: "A fountain of gardens, a well of living waters, and flowing streams" etc. (Song 4:15). And it also says: "Drink waters out of thine own cistern, and running waters out of thine own well" (Prov. 5:15).

46. *The Stubborn Caretaker; anonymous; Mek. Beshallach 5:58–79*

"And Moses stretched out his hand over the sea" (Exod. 14:21). Immediately the sea began to withstand him. Moses ordered it in the name of the Holy One, blessed be He, to divide itself, but it would not submit. Moses then showed it the staff, but still it refused to yield.

A parable. Unto what is the matter like? It is like a king[24] who had two gardens, one inside the other. He sold the inner one, but when the buyer came wishing to enter the inner garden, the keeper would not let him. The buyer spoke to the keeper in the name of the king, but the keeper would not yield. He then showed him the king's ring, and still he refused to yield. So the buyer had to go and bring the king himself with him. As soon as the buyer came, conducting the king, the keeper started to run away. The buyer then called out to him: The whole day I have been speaking to you in the

---

[24]Lauterbach: To give a parable, to what is the matter like? To a king.

name of the king,[25] but you would not accept it; and now why are you running away? The keeper answered him: It is not on account of you that I am fleeing; it is on account of the king.

Even so, Moses came and stood by the sea. He told it[26] in the name of the Holy One, blessed be He, to divide itself, but it would not consent. He showed it the staff, but it would not consent,[27] until the Holy One, blessed be He, revealed Himself over it in His glory. And as soon as the Holy One, blessed be He, revealed Himself in His might and His glory, the sea began to flee, as it is said: "The sea saw it and fled" (Ps. 114:3). Moses then said to it: All day long I have been talking to you in the name of the Holy One, blessed be He, and you would not listen, and now wherefore are you fleeing? "What aileth thee, O thou sea, that thou fleest?" (Ps. 114:5). The sea answered him: It is not because of you, Moses, it is not because of you, son of Amram. It is only because: "Tremble, thou earth, at the presence of the Lord, and the presence of the God of Jacob; who turned the rock into a pool of water, the flint into a fountain of waters" (Ps. 114:7–8).

47. *The Two Dutiful Sons; R. Meir; ca. 150; Mek. Beshallach 6:8–22*

[R. Meir and R. Judah (b. Ilai) differ in their versions of who stepped into the sea (Exod. 14:22) first and under what circumstances. R. Meir argues that it was the tribe of Benjamin and supports his argument with a parable.]

A parable. Unto what is the matter like? It is like a king[28] who had two sons, one grown up and the other still young. He said to the young one: Wake me at sunrise. And to the older one he said: Wake me after three hours of the morning. When the young one came to wake him at sunrise, the older would not let him, saying: He told me to wake him only after three hours of the morning. And the younger one said to him: But he told me: At sunrise. While they were standing

---

[25] Lauterbach: I have been telling you the order of the king.

[26] Lauterbach: So also when Moses came and stood by the sea, ordering it.

[27] Lauterbach: and still it refused to consent.

[28] Lauterbach: To give a parable, to what is this like? To a king.

there wrangling with each other, their father woke up. He said to them: My sons, after all, both of you had only my honor in mind. So I will not withhold your reward from you.

Likewise, what reward did the tribe of Benjamin receive for going down to the sea first? The Shekinah rested in his portion of the land, as it is said: "Benjamin is a wolf that raveneth" (Gen. 49:27). And it also says: "Of Benjamin He said: The beloved of the Lord shall dwell in safety by Him" (Deut. 33:12). And what reward did the tribe of Judah receive? It merited royalty, as it is said: "The princes of Judah with their royalty [*rigmatam*]" (Ps. 68:28). For the word *rigmah* merely alludes to royalty, as it is said: "Then commanded Belshazzar, and they clothed Daniel with purple ['*argewana* = '*argeman*]," etc. (Dan. 5:29).

48. *The Dove, the Hawk, and the King; anonymous; Mek. Beshallach 7:27–36*

"And the Egyptians fled against it" (Exod. 14:27). This teaches that in whatever direction an Egyptian fled, the sea would be rushing against him.

A parable. Unto what is the matter like? It is like a dove[29] that flees from a hawk and enters the palace of the king. The king opens the eastern window for her, and she goes out and flies away. When the hawk, pursuing her, enters the palace, the king shuts all the windows and begins shooting arrows at him.

Even so,[30] when the last of the Israelites came out from the sea, the last of the pursuing Egyptians entered into the bed of the sea. The ministering angels then began hurling at them arrows, great hailstones, fire and brimstone, as it is said: "And I will plead against him with pestilence and with blood . . . and great hailstones, fire and brimstone" (Ezek. 38:22).

---

[29]Lauterbach: To give a parable, to what can this be compared? To a dove.
[30]Lauterbach: So also.

49. The Lame and Blind Caretakers; R. Judah ha-Nasi; ca. 200; Mek. Shirata 2:130–33 (cf. B. Sanhedrin 91a–b; Lev. R. 4:5)

Antoninus asked our teacher, the saint: After a man has died and his body ceased to be, does God then make him stand trial? He answered him: Rather than ask about the body that is impure, ask me about the soul that is pure.

They parable a parable. Unto what is the matter like? It is like a king[31] of flesh and blood who had a beautiful orchard [pardes]. The king placed in it two keepers, one of whom was lame and the other blind. [At this point all manuscripts of Mekilta abbreviate the parable by omitting everything until the end of it, apparently considering it too familiar a story to repeat in its entirety; we therefore complete it from the parallel in the Babylonian Talmud.] The lame man said to the blind: I see beautiful figs in the orchard. Come and take me upon thy shoulder, that we may procure and eat them. So the lame man bestrode the blind, procured and ate them. Some time after, the owner of the orchard came and said to them: Where are those beautiful figs? The lame man replied: Have I then feet to walk with? The blind man replied: Have I then eyes to see with? What did he do? He placed the lame upon the blind and judged them both together as one.

Also will the Holy One, blessed be He, bring the soul, replace it in the body, and judge them together, as it is written: "He shall call to the heavens from above, and to the earth, that He may judge His people" (Ps. 50:4). "He shall call to the heavens from above"—this refers to the soul; "and to the earth, that He may judge His people"—to the body.

[The illustrand in the talmudic parallel (B. Sanhedrin 91 a–b) that we have used to fill out the version in Mekilta is significantly different and worth quoting in full: "Antoninus said to Rabbi: The body and soul can both free themselves from judgment. Thus the body can plead: The soul has sinned, (the proof being that) from the day it left me I lie like a dumb stone in the grave. And the soul can say: The body

---

[31]Lauterbach: To give a parable for this, to what is this like? To the following: A king.

has sinned, (the proof being that) from the day I departed from it I fly about in the air like a bird." Antoninus figures in many stories as the prototypical good Gentile and, according to some, an eventual proselyte. The Roman emperor Antoninus Pius (138–61 C.E.) repealed the severe laws that his predecessor, Hadrian, had decreed against the practice of Judaism, following the Bar Cochba revolt.]

50. *A King and His Entourage; perhaps R. Eliezer b. Hyrcanus; ca. 90; Mek. Shirata 3:28–39*

"This is my God, and I will glorify Him" (Exod. 15:2). R. Eliezer says: Whence can you say that a maidservant saw at the sea what Isaiah and Ezekiel and all the prophets never saw? It says about them: "And by the ministry of the prophets have I used similitudes" (Hos. 12:10). And it is also written: "The heavens were opened, and I saw visions of God" (Ezek. 1:1).

They parable a parable. Unto what is the matter like? It is like a king of flesh and blood who enters[32] a province surrounded by a circle of guards. His heroes stand to the right of him and to the left of him. His soldiers are before him and behind him. And all the people ask, saying: Which one is the king? Because he is of flesh and blood like those who surround him.

But when the Holy One, blessed be He, revealed Himself at the sea, no one had to ask: Which one is the king? But as soon as they saw Him, they recognized Him, and they all opened their mouths and said: "This is my God, and I will glorify Him."

51. *The Accompanying Father; anonymous; Mek. Shirata 3:65–74*

[Commenting on Song 2:16:] And the other sages say: I will accompany Him until I come with Him into His temple.

A parable. It is like a king who had a son[33] who went

---

[32]Lauterbach: To give a parable for this, to what is this like? To the following: A king enters.

[33]Lauterbach: To give a parable, a king had a son.

away to a far country. He went after him and stood by him. Then the son went to another country, and the king again followed him and stood by him.

Even so,[34] when Israel went down to Egypt, the Shekinah went down with them, as it is said: "And I will surely bring thee up again" (Gen. 46:4). When they went into the sea, the Shekinah was with them, as it is said: "And the angel of God . . . removed," etc. (Exod. 14:19). When they went out into the wilderness the Shekinah was with them, as it is said, "And the Lord went before them by day (13:21) until they brought Him with them to His holy temple. And so it also says: "Scarce had I passed from them" etc. (Song 3:4).

52. *The Ashamed Bridegroom; anonymous; Mek. Shirata 3:78–84*

"My father's God, and I will exalt Him" (Exod. 15:2). I am a queen, the daughter of kings; beloved, the daughter of beloved ones; holy, the daughter of holy ones; pure, the daughter of pure ones.

A parable. It is like a man who goes forth[35] to betroth a woman. Sometimes he may be ashamed of her, sometimes he may be ashamed of her family, sometimes he may be ashamed of her relatives.

But I am not thus.[36] Rather, I am a queen, the daughter of kings; beloved, the daughter of beloved ones; holy, the daughter of holy ones; pure, the daughter of pure ones.

53. *The Cruel Robber's Designs; anonymous; Mek. Shirata 7:57–65*

[Discussion of the plans and boasts of the Egyptians regarding what they would do to the Israelites.]

They parable a parable. Unto what is the matter like? It is like a robber who was standing behind the king's palace

---

[34]Lauterbach: So also.

[35]Lauterbach: To give a parable: A man goes forth.

[36]Lauterbach: I, however, am not of that kind.

and hurling imprecations. He says:[37] If I find the prince, I shall seize him, I shall kill him, I shall crucify him, I shall make him die the most cruel death.

Even so[38] did the wicked Pharaoh stand and hurl imprecations in the land of Egypt: "The enemy said: I will pursue, I will overtake" etc. (Exod. 15:9). But the Holy Spirit laughs at him and says: "Thou didst blow with thy wind" (v. 10). And it also says: "Thou stretchest out thy right hand" (v. 12). And it also says: "Why are the nations in an uproar. . . . Let us break their bands asunder. . . . He that sitteth in heaven laugheth" (Ps. 2:1–4).

54. *The Fragility of Eggs; anonymous; Mek. Shirata 9:20–23*

[Following a series of Scriptures indicating how God stretches out His hand to destroy.]

A parable. Unto what is the matter like? It is like eggs that are placed in a man's hand, so if he but turn[39] his hand a little they all fall and break.

For it is said: "So when the Lord shall stretch out His hand, both he that helped shall stumble, and he that is helped shall fall" etc. (Isa. 31:3).

55. *The Defeated Robbers; anonymous; Mek. Shirata 10:42–49*

"The Lord shall reign" (Exod. 15:18). When? When Thou wilt again build it with both Thy hands.

A parable. Unto what is the matter like? It is like robbers who entered[40] the palace of a king, despoiled his property, killed the royal household, and destroyed the palace of the king. After some time, however, the king sat in judgment over them. Some of them he imprisoned, some of them he killed, some of them he crucified. He then again dwelt in his palace. And therefore his reign was recognized in the world.

---

[37] Lauterbach: To give a parable, to what can this be compared? To the following: A robber standing behind the king's palace, defiantly says.

[38] Lauterbach: So also.

[39] Lauterbach: To give a parable, to what is this like? To this: When eggs are placed in a man's hand, if he but turn.

[40] Lauterbach: To give a parable, to what is this to be compared? To the following: Robbers entered.

In this sense it is said: "The sanctuary, O Lord, that Thy hands have established. The Lord shall reign for ever and ever" (Exod. 15:17–18).

[The verse being commented upon is in Miriam's song of triumph over the Egyptians, but the mention of the sanctuary appears to have brought something else into the parabler's mind: the destruction of the temple, either by the Babylonians or by the Romans. There are some similarities to no. 53.]

56. *The Banished Prince; perhaps R. Eleazar of Modiim; ca. 140; Mek. Amelek 2:16–28 (cf. Sifre on Numbers 134; Sifre on Deuteronomy 29)*

[Comments on Exod. 17:14.] R. Eleazar of Modiim says: This is one of the four cases of righteous men to whom a hint was given. Two of them apprehended and two did not. Moses was given a hint, but he did not apprehend it. . . . Whence do we know about Moses? It is said: "And rehearse it in the ears of Joshua." God thereby as much as told him: Joshua will lead Israel to inherit the land. And yet in the end, Moses was still standing and beseeching, as it is said: "And I besought the Lord" etc. (Deut. 3:23).

A parable. It is like a king[41] who decreed against his son that the son should not come unto him into his palace. The son entered the first gate, and the guards kept their peace. He entered the second gate, and again the guards kept their peace. But at the third gate they rebuked him and said to him: It is enough for you to have come so far.

Even so,[42] when Moses conquered the lands of the two nations, the land of Sihon and the land of Og, and gave it to the tribe of Reuben and the tribe of Manasseh, the people said to him: It seems as if the decree against you was not unconditional. Maybe we likewise have not been sentenced unconditionally.

---

[41]Lauterbach: To give a parable, this may be compared to the case of a king.

[42]Lauterbach: So also was it.

57. The Beneficent King; anonymous; Mek. Bachodesh 5:1–11

"I am the Lord thy God" (Exod. 20:2). Why were the Ten Commandments not said at the beginning of the Torah?

They parable a parable. Unto what is the matter like? It is like a king[43] who entered a province and said to the people: May I be your king? But the people said to him: Have you done anything good for us that you should rule over us? What did he do then? He built the city wall for them, he brought in the water supply for them, and he fought their battles. Then he said to them: May I be your king? And they said to him: Yes, yes.[44]

Likewise God: He brought the Israelites out of Egypt, divided the sea for them, sent down the manna for them, brought up the well for them, brought the quails for them. He fought for them the battle with Amalek. Then He said to them: I am to be your King. And they said to Him: Yes, yes.

Rabbi says: This proclaims the excellence of Israel. . . .

58. The Two Administrators; R. Simon b. Eleazar; ca. 170; Mek. Bachodesh 5:81–92

R. Simeon b. Eleazar says: If the sons of Noah could not endure the seven commandments enjoined upon them, how much less could they have endured all the commandments of the Torah!

A parable. It is like a king who appointed two administrators [epitropoi].[45] One was appointed over the store of straw, and the other was appointed over the treasure of silver and gold. The one appointed over the store of straw was held in suspicion. But he used to complain about the fact that they had not appointed him over the treasure of silver and gold. They said to him: Fool [reka]![46] If you were under suspicion in connection with the affair concerning straw,

---

[43]Lauterbach: They give a parable. To what may this be compared? To the following: A king.

[44]Lauterbach: Then when he said to them: May I be your king? They said to him: Yes, yes.

[45]Lauterbach: To give a parable. A king had appointed two administrators.

[46]Lauterbach writes only "Reka!"

how could they trust you with the treasure of silver and gold?

Behold, it is a matter of reasoning by the method of *qal ve-chomer:* If the sons of Noah could not endure the seven commandments enjoined upon them, how much less could they have endured all the commandments of the Torah!

[In classical rabbinic doctrine it was taught that God gave to Adam certain laws, traditionally six in number— prohibition of idolatry, blasphemy, murder, sexual impurity, and theft and the commandment to set up courts of justice. To Noah was given a seventh commandment—not to eat a limb torn from a living animal and not to eat blood (Gen. 9:4). These seven Noachian laws were binding upon all peoples, but only to Israel were given the laws of Sinai. Frequently one encounters in the rabbinic literature Greek technical terms such as *epitropoi.* The Aramaic *reka* (empty-head, idiot) is the same word cited by Jesus in Matt. 5:22. *Qal ve-chomer* (light and heavy) was the most important rule of rabbinic exegesis; it means reasoning from minor to major or vice versa. This method is used in the New Testament, for example, in John 7:23.]

59. *The Patient King; anonymous; Mek. Bachodesh 6:1–17*

"Thou shalt not have other gods before Me" (Exod. 20:3). Why is this said? Because it says: "I am the Lord thy God" (v. 2).

A parable. It is like a king of flesh and blood who entered[47] a province. His attendants said to him: Issue some decrees upon them. He said unto them: No! When they have accepted my reign, I shall issue decrees upon them. For if they do not accept my reign, how will they carry out my decrees?

Even so,[48] God said to Israel: "I am the Lord thy God; thou shalt not have other gods"—I am He whose reign you have taken upon yourselves in Egypt. And then they said to Him: Yes, yes. He said: Now, just as you have accepted My reign, you must also accept My decrees: "Thou shalt not have other gods before Me."

---

[47]Lauterbach: To give a parable: A king of flesh and blood entered.
[48]Lauterbach: Likewise.

[While no. 57 explains the relationship of the Decalogue to the material that precedes it, no. 59 explains the relationship of Exod. 20:3 to the verse that precedes it.]

60–61. *The Dog Named After Father, The King Going Out to War; R. Gamaliel II; ca. 80; Mek. Bachodesh 6:103–24 (cf. B. Abodah Zarah 54b–55a)*

[60] A certain philosopher asked R. Gamaliel: It is written in your Torah: "For I the Lord thy God am a jealous God" (Exod. 20:5). But is there any power in the idol that it should arouse jealousy? A hero is jealous of another hero, a wise man is jealous of another wise man, a rich man is jealous of another rich man, but has the idol any power that one should be jealous of it?

R. Gamaliel said to him: Suppose a man would call his dog by the name of his father, so that when taking a vow, he would vow: By the life of this dog. Against whom would the father be incensed? Against the son or the dog?

[61] Said the philosopher to him: Some idols are worthwhile. R. Gamaliel said: What makes you think so? Said the philosopher: There raged a fire in a certain city, but the temple of the idol in it was saved. Was it not because the idol could take care of itself?

R. Gamaliel said to him: I will parable to thee a parable. Unto what is the matter like? It is like a king of flesh and blood who goes out to war.[49] Against whom does he wage war, against the living or against the dead?

He said to him: With the living. (Then) he said:[50] But if there is no usefulness in any of them, why does He not annihilate them? R. Gamaliel said: But is it only one object that you worship? Behold, you worship the sun, the moon, the stars, and the planets, the mountains and the hills, the springs and the glens, and even human beings. Shall He destroy His world because of fools? "Shall I utterly consume all things from off the face of the earth? saith the Lord"

---

[49]Lauterbach: Said R. Gamaliel to him: I will give you a parable: To what is this comparable? To the conduct of a king of flesh and blood when he goes out to war.

[50]Lauterbach: The philosopher then said: "Indeed, only against the living." Then he said again.

(Zeph. 1:2). The philosopher said to him: Since it causes the wicked to stumble, why does God not remove it from the world? But R. Gamaliel said: Because of fools? If so, then since they also worship human beings, "Shall I cut off man from the face of the earth" (v. 3)?

62. The King's Portraits Defaced; R. Hanina b. Gamaliel; ca. 85; Mek. Bachodesh 8:69–77

How were the Ten Commandments arranged? Five on the one tablet, and five on the other. On the one tablet was written: "I am the Lord thy God." And opposite it on the other tablet was written: "Thou shalt not murder." This tells that if one sheds blood, it is accounted to him as though he diminished the divine image.

A parable. It is like a king of flesh and blood who entered a province,[51] and the people set up portraits of him, made images of him, and struck coins in his honor. Later on, they upset his portraits, broke his images, and defaced his coins, thus diminishing the likenesses of the king.

Even so is everyone who sheds blood: It is accounted to him as though he had diminished the divine image, as it is said: "Whosoever sheddeth man's blood . . . for in the image of God made He man" (Gen. 9:6).

[This pericope begins a coherent exposition of the Decalogue that as a unit is attributed to R. Hananiah (or Hanina) b. Gamaliel. His view (which resembles that of Philo) is contrasted with that of the majority of the sages, who held that all ten commandments were on each table (Mek. Bachodesh 8:98ff.)].

63. The Partner with a Thief; R. Simeon b. Yohai; ca. 140; Mek. Nezikin 13:79–88 (cf. Tos. Baba Kamma 7:13)

R. Simeon b. Yohai says: Behold it says: "Whoso is partner with a thief hateth his own soul: he heareth the adjuration and uttereth nothing" (Prov. 29:24).

They parable a parable. Unto what is the matter like? It

---

[51]Lauterbach: To give a parable: A king of flesh and blood entered a province.

is like one who comes out from another's house[52] carrying away a load of things. A friend of his meets him and says to him: What are you doing? He says: Take your share and do not tell on me. After a while the owner of the stolen articles comes and says to the friend of the thief: I adjure you, tell me, have you not seen so-and-so coming out from my house and carrying away a load of things? He says: I swear that I do not know what you are talking about.

Behold, such a one forfeits his life and to him applies the verse: "Whoso is partner with a thief hateth his own soul."

SIFRA ON LEVITICUS

Sifra, a halakic midrash on Leviticus, is a collection of Tannaitic sayings that was probably compiled and arranged in its present form after the end of the fourth century C.E. Out of eleven items we present seven.

64. *The Mother Who Substituted for Her Daughter; anonymous; Sifra on Lev. 8:15*

"And Moses killed it and took the blood" (Lev. 8:15). . . . . All seven days Moses carried out the duties of the high priest. He slaughtered, he threw (the blood), he sprinkled, he poured out, he made atonement. Therefore it says: "And he killed, and Moses took. . . ."

A parable. Unto what is the matter like? It is like a king's daughter who was married when she was very young, and it was arranged that her mother should carry out the household duties until her daughter had learned them.

So also Aaron. At first he was a Levite. For it says: "Is there not Aaron, your brother, the Levite?" (Exod. 4:14). However, when he was chosen to be High Priest, the Holy One, blessed be He, said to Moses: You shall perform My service until Aaron has learned how. Moses sacrificed, and Aaron watched. He threw, and Aaron watched. He sprinkled, and he watched. He purified, and he watched. He poured out, and he watched. He made atonement, and he watched.

---

[52]Lauterbach: They illustrate this by the following parable: One comes out from another man's house.

65. *The Restored Wife; anonymous; Sifra on Lev. 9:4–5*

"For today the Lord will appear to you. And they brought what Moses commanded. And all the congregation drew near and stood before the Lord" (Lev. 9:4–5). They all came with haste and stood before the Lord.

A parable. It is like a king who was provoked with his wife and sent her away. Then after a time he was reconciled to her. Immediately she girded up her loins, fastened her garments about her shoulders, and served him even more than was necessary.

So also the Israelites. When they saw that God was well disposed to forgive their sins, they hastened with joy and presented themselves before Him. Therefore it says: "And all the congregation drew near and stood before the Lord."

66. *The Shy Bride; anonymous; Sifra on Lev. 9:6–7*

"Then Moses said to Aaron: Draw near to the altar" (Lev. 9:7).

A parable. Unto what is the matter like? It is like a king of flesh and blood who had married a wife. She, however, was shy in his presence, and her sister went with her to the king. Then she said to her: For what reason did you enter into this relation? Was it not to serve the king? Take courage now and come serve the king.

Even so Moses said to Aaron: Aaron, my brother, for what purpose were you selected? Was it not in order that you might serve before the Holy One? Take courage now and set about your duties. And some said: To Aaron the altar had the form of an ox, and he was afraid before it. But Moses said to him: It is not anything before which you are accustomed to be terrified. Take courage and approach the altar. Therefore it says: "Draw near to the altar."

67. *The Prince's Indigestion; anonymous; Sifra on Lev. 18:28*

"Lest the land vomit you out, when you defile it" (Lev. 18:28). The land of Israel is not like other lands. It does not retain the evildoer.

They parable a parable. Unto what is the matter like? It is like a king's son to whom someone gave food that was not suited to his stomach. He then vomited it out.

Even so is the land of Israel. It does not retain the evildoer. Therefore it says: "Lest the land vomit you out, when you defile it, as it vomited out the nation that was before you."

[There is a partial parallel in no. 92.]

68. *The Exceptional Laborer; anonymous; Sifra on Lev. 26:9 (cf. Eccl. R. 5:11:5)*

"And I will have regard for you" (Lev. 26:9).

They parable a parable. Unto what is the matter like? It is like a king who hired many laborers. And along with them was one laborer that had worked for him many days. All the laborers went to receive their pay for the day, and this one special laborer went also. He said to this one special laborer: I will have regard for you. The others, who have worked for me only a little, to them I will give small pay. You, however, will receive a large recompense.

Even so both the Israelites and the peoples of the world sought their pay from God. And God said to the Israelites: My children, I will have regard for you. The peoples of the world have accomplished very little for Me, and I will give them but a small reward. You, however, will receive a large recompense. Therefore it says: "And I will have regard for you."

[There is some similarity between this parable and that told by the Amora R. Zeira at the funeral of Abun b. Hiya (P. Berakoth 2:8; Song R. 6:2:6); it is interesting to compare and contrast both rabbinic parables with Matt. 20:1–16.]

69. *The Egalitarian King; anonymous; Sifra on Lev. 26:11*

"And I will make my abode among you" (Lev. 26:11).

They parable a parable. Unto what is the matter like? It is like a king who went out to walk about with his gardener. The gardener, however, hid himself from the king. The king said to the gardener: Why do you have to hide from me? Behold, I am one like you.

Even so, someday will the Holy One, blessed be He, walk about with the pious in the Garden of Eden. And the pious see Him and tremble before Him. But the Holy One, blessed be He, says to the pious: Why do you tremble before Me? Behold, I am one like yourselves.

70. *The Abused Ox; anonymous; Sifra on Lev. 26:13 (cf. Midrash on Ps. 129:1)*

"I have broken the bars of your yoke" (Lev. 26:13).

They parable a parable. Unto what is the matter like? It is like a householder who had an ox used for plowing, and he loaned him to another. This man, however, had ten sons. First one came and plowed with the ox and then took his rest, and then another came and plowed with the ox and took his rest, until the ox was completely exhausted and lay down unable to move. Then all the oxen went home, but this one ox could not go home. He [the ox's owner] was not content to accept soothing apologies from the man, but instead he came immediately and broke the yoke and chopped up the yoke bar.

Even so is Israel in this world. One conqueror comes and forces Israel under the yoke. And the roll of the conquerors is long. For it says: "The plowers plowed upon my back: they made long furrows" (Ps. 129:3). In the future when the end comes, the Holy One, blessed be He, will not say to the peoples: You have done such and such to My people. Rather He comes immediately and breaks the yoke and chops up the yoke bar. For it says: "I have broken the bars of your yoke."

SIFRE ON NUMBERS

The Sifre on the legal portions of Numbers was probably arranged and edited in Palestine soon after the end of the fourth century C.E. Of twenty-five parabolic items we here present fourteen.

71. *The Viceroy as Advance Man; R. Simeon b. Yohai; ca. 140; Sifre on Numbers 82*

"And the ark of the covenant of the Lord went before them" (Num. 10:33). This ark that went with them into the camp contained the broken tablets (of the law).

R. Simeon b. Yohai says: A parable. It is like a viceroy [*antecaesar*] who went before his armies to prepare for them a place where they should camp.

So the Shekinah went before Israel and prepared for them a place where they should dwell.

72. *The Brazen Curser of the King; R. Simeon b. Yohai; ca. 140; Sifre on Numbers 85*

"In the ears of the Lord" (Num. 11:1). This suggests that the Israelites intended to make God Himself hear (their complaints).

R. Simeon says: A parable. Unto what is the matter like? It is like one who was cursing the king, and when the king passed by, the people said to the offender: Hush, lest the king hear thee! He said: How do you know that I did not intend that he should hear?

73. *The Son Who Sought an Intercessor; R. Simeon b. Yohai; ca. 140; Sifre on Numbers 86*

"And the people cried to Moses" (Num. 11:2). But how could Moses help them? It ought to have been said of them: And they cried unto the Lord!

R. Simeon says: A parable. Unto what is the matter like? It is like a king who got angry with his son, and the son went to one of his father's friends and said to him: Go and intercede with my father for me.

Even so the children of Israel went to Moses and said: Intercede with God for us.

[This parable is partially parallel to no. 44, but it depicts an earlier scene in the action. Here the son seeks a mediator,

but in the other parable the mediator is already interceding
with the king.]

74. *The Son Ungrateful for His Food; R. Simeon b. Yohai;
ca. 140; Sifre on Numbers 87*

"We remember the fish that we did eat in Egypt for
nothing, the cucumbers" etc. (Num. 11:5). R. Simeon says:
The manna tasted according to their fancy, except for these
five kinds of food [mentioned in the passage—melons,
cucumbers, leeks, onions, and garlic].

A parable. It is like a king of flesh and blood who sent
his son to a tutor (pedagogue) and charged him saying: See
that my son does not eat bad food or drink bad drinks. But
the son murmured against the father, saying: Not because he
loves me, but because he does not wish me to eat, has he
ordered this.

The sages say: The manna tasted according to their
fancy, but they saw only manna, as it is said: "Our soul is
dried away, there is nothing at all save this manna to look
upon" (Num. 11:6).

[This is one of several parables in which one of the
characters is a "tutor," which is the word we have used to
translate *piydagog*, the Hebraized form of Greek *paidagōgos*.
The same Greek word is used in Gal. 3:24.]

75. *The King Who Made His Son Dependent; R. Simeon b.
Yohai; ca. 140; Sifre on Numbers 89*

R. Simeon says: Why did not the manna come down on
Israel once a year? In order that their hearts should be turned
to their Father who is in heaven.

A parable. Unto what is the matter like? It is like a king
who decided to supply his son with food once a year, for the
whole year. The son did not meet (receive the countenance
of) his father, except at that time when he received from him
his allowance. Then the father changed his mind and
decided to feed his son once a day. (Thus the son became
more dependent upon his father for his daily sustenance.)

And the son said: I shall meet my father once a day, it is enough.

So in Israel: a man having five boys or girls would sit and keep watch, saying: Woe is me! Perhaps the manna will not come down tomorrow, and we shall die of starvation! May it be Thy will that it should come down. And thus their hearts were turned to heaven.

76. The Man Who Accompanied His Sons to Execution; R. Simeon b. Yohai; ca. 140; Sifre on Numbers 91 (cf. B. Yoma 76a)

"I am not able to bear all this people alone, for it is too heavy for me, and if Thou deal thus with me, kill me, I pray Thee, out of hand" (Num. 11:14–15). It is because the Holy One, blessed is He, showed Moses all the punishments that He would bring upon them.

R. Simeon says: A parable. Unto what is the matter like? It is like one who accompanied his sons to their execution. He said to the executioner: Kill me, before thou killest my children! (Not as it is said concerning Zedekiah, "The king of Babylon slew the sons of Zedekiah before his eyes," and afterward "he put out the eyes of Zedekiah" [Jer. 52:10–11].)

Even so Moses said to God: If that is what will happen to my people, better kill me; it is better for me that Thou shouldest kill me first, so that I should not see the sorrows that will come upon them.

77. The Tender-Minded Father; anonymous; Sifre on Numbers 105

"And the cloud was removed from over the tent" (Num. 12:10).

A parable. It is like a king who said to the tutor (pedagogue) of his son: Chastise my son, but not until I have gone away. For the father was full of pity for his son.

Now, if God, even in the hour of His anger, is full of pity for the righteous, how much more so in the "acceptable time" (Isa. 49:8)?

[For "tutor," see the notes under nos. 74 and 99.]

78. *The Son Who Was Slave by Redemption; anonymous; Sifre on Numbers 115*

Another explanation. Why, at every performance of a commandment, must we have the Exodus in our thoughts?

A parable. It is like a king whose friend's son was taken prisoner. The king redeemed him, but expressly upon the understanding that he should become the king's slave, so that at any time, if he should disobey the king, the latter could say: Thou art my slave! As soon as they came into a country, the king said to him: Put my sandals on for me! Take my clothes to the bathhouse! That son began to protest. And the king took out the bill of sale and said to him: Thou art my slave!

So when the Holy One, blessed be He, redeemed the descendants of Abraham, His beloved friend, He did not redeem them with the view that they should be (His) sons, but (His) slaves, in order that when He commands and they do not obey, He could say to them: Ye are My slaves! And as soon as they went out into the desert, He began to issue some light commandments, and some weighty ones—for instance, the laws of the Sabbath and incest (grave ones), of the fringes and the phylacteries (light ones). Then the Israelites began to protest. He said to them: Ye are My slaves! For this reason have I redeemed you, that I might give decrees and ye should keep them.

79. *The Unregistered Donation; anonymous; Sifre on Numbers 117 (cf. ibid. 119)*

"I have given thee the contribution, even all the holy things of the children of Israel" (Num. 18:8). Scripture (God) made a covenant with Aaron concerning all the most holy things, a decree and a covenant, because Korah stood up against him and contested (his) priesthood.

A parable. Unto what is the matter like? It is like a king who had a minister to whom he made a present of a field, but he neither wrote nor sealed a deed of donation, nor did he enter it in the recorder's office. One day, a certain person came and contested the minister's right to the field. Then said the king: Anyone who chooses can now deny thy right to the field! Come, I will write out (a deed of donation). I will sign it and enter it in the recorder's office.

Therefore this section is close to the section about Korah.

[The parallel attributes the parable to R. Ishmael b. Elisha, ca. 130.]

80. *The Foolish Deserter; R. Akiba; ca. 130; Sifre on Numbers 131*

"And the daughter of any priest, if she profane herself by playing the whore . . . shall be burned with fire" (Lev. 21:9), and immediately after it, "And if the high priest" (v. 10). R. Akiba said: There is a connection, for when a priest's daughter is burned for immorality, a high priest is, so to speak, burned with her.

A parable. Unto what is the matter like? It is like a centurion who had served his term but failed to enter his primipilate (to which he would have been promoted in due time) and fled. The king sent after him, and when he was brought back, the king commanded that the head of the deserter be cut off. Before the execution, the king said: Fill a casket with golden dinars and carry it before him, and say unto him: If thou hadst behaved like thy colleagues, thou wouldst have received the basket of golden dinars and (preserved) thy soul, but now thou hast lost thy soul and thou hast lost thy money.

Even so is the daughter of a priest (who has gone astray): the high priest goes in front of her and says to her: If thou hadst behaved in the way in which thy mother behaved, thou mightest have been found worthy to become the ancestress of a high priest like me, but now thou hast lost thyself and also thy honor.

[In the Roman military system *primipilus* was the highest rank to which a centurion could be promoted.]

81. *The King Repenting His Intention to Divorce; probably R. Akiba; ca. 130; Sifre on Numbers 131*

Similarly it says: "For ye are not My people" (Hos. 1:9); and (immediately afterward) it says: "And the number of the children of Israel shall be as the sand of the sea, which cannot be measured or numbered; and it shall come to pass that in the place where it was said unto them: Ye are not My people, there it shall be said unto them: Ye are the sons of the living God" (v. 10). What connection is there between these verses?

It is like a king who, being angry with his wife, sent for a scribe to come and write for her a bill of divorcement. But before the scribe arrived, the king was again reconciled with his wife. Said the king: Should the scribe go back as soon as he has come, without having done anything? Therefore he said to him: Come and write that I have doubled her dowry.

82. *Mercy for a Rebellious Province; either Akiba or anonymous; Sifre on Numbers 131 (cf. Pesikta de Rab Kahana 24:11)*

Similarly it says: "Samaria must be condemned, for she hath rebelled against her God" (Hos. 13:16 [MT 14:1]); and (immediately afterward) it says: "O Israel, return unto the Lord thy God" (14:1 [MT v. 2]). What is the connection?

A parable. Unto what is the matter like? It is like a province that rebelled against its king. The king sent out a general with orders to devastate that province. That general was experienced and cool-headed. He said to them: Take heed! Otherwise I will do unto you as I have done unto such and such a province, and with such and such a government.

Therefore it says: "Samaria must be condemned, for she has rebelled against her God," and (immediately afterward): "Return, O Israel."

83. *Divine and Human Justice; R. Judah b. Baba; ca. 130; Sifre on Numbers 134*

"Who is there in heaven or earth a god?" (Deut. 3:24). That means: the way of God [lit., "the Place"] is not like that of flesh and blood. The nature and way of flesh and blood is as follows: Whoever is more powerful than the other can annul the latter's plans. But Thou—who is able to turn Thy hand aside? And in this sense it says: "But He is unchangeable, and who can turn Him?" (Job 23:13).

R. Judah b. Baba said: A parable. It is like a man who is involved in a case before the Roman government. He can pay as much gold as he likes, but he still cannot disentangle himself.

But Thou, on the other hand, sayest: Repent, and I will accept you. For it says: "I have swept away your transgressions like a cloud" (Isa. 44:22).

84. *The Wise Sheep Dogs; anonymous; Sifre on Numbers 137 (cf. B. Sanhedrin 105a)*

"The Lord said to Moses: Avenge the people of Israel on the Midianites" (Num. 31:1–2). . . . But notice that the Moabites had begun the trouble. For it says: "So the elders of Moab and the elders of Midian departed" (22:7). Never previously had these two nations been at peace; but as they went out against Israel, they made peace with one another in order to fight Israel.

A parable. Unto what is the matter like? It is like two dogs that were with a sheep herd and were continually quarreling. Then a wolf came to steal a lamb from the flock, and one of the dogs started to attack him. The other dog said to himself: If I don't go to his assistance now, then the wolf will kill him and later attack and kill me. So the two made peace and together attacked the wolf.

So also Moab and Midian had never previously been at peace. For it says: "Who defeated Midian in the country of Moab" (Gen. 36:35). As they set out to make war with Israel, however, they made peace with one another and made war with Israel. ↙

SIFRE ON DEUTERONOMY

Sifre on Deuteronomy, compiled in the late fourth century and considered to be from the School of Akiba, resembles Mekilta of Simeon b. Yohai. Many of the parables in it are attributed to Simeon. Out of some forty-three parabolic items gleaned from the work, we here present twenty-two.

85. *The Improved Field; anonymous; Sifre on Deuteronomy 8*

"Which the Lord swore to your fathers" (Deut. 1:8). There was no need for it to say "to Abraham, Isaac, and Jacob." But what does it teach, that it does add to "Abraham, Isaac, and Jacob"? Worthy is Abraham by himself alone; worthy is Isaac by himself alone; worthy is Jacob by himself alone.

A parable. It is like a king who gave to his servant a field as a present, and he gave it to him just as it was. Then the servant set to work and improved it and said: See what I have now? He gave it to me just as it was. Then he went and planted a vineyard on the land and said: See what I have now? He gave it to me just as it was.

Even so the Holy One, blessed be He, gave the land to Abraham our father just as it was, as it says: "Arise, walk through the length and the breadth of the land, for I will give it to you" (Gen. 13:17). Then Abraham went out and improved the land, as it says: "And Abraham planted a tamarisk tree in Beersheba" (21:33). Then Isaac went out and improved the land, as it says: "And Isaac sowed in the land, and reaped in the same year a hundredfold" (26:12). And then Jacob went out and carried out improvements, as it says: "And he bought the piece of land on which he had pitched his tent" (33:19).

86. *The Great Inheritance; anonymous; Sifre on Deuteronomy 19 (cf. ibid. 356)*

"You have come to the hill country of the Amorites, which the Lord our God gives us" (Deut. 1:20).

A parable. It is like a king who turned his son over to a tutor (pedagogue). The latter led him around and pointed everything out to him and said to him: All these grapevines are yours, and all these vineyards and all these olive orchards are yours. But when he was exhausted with looking at everything, then he said to him: Everything that you see is yours.

Even so was Israel. When they were in the wilderness forty years, Moses said to them: "For the Lord your God is bringing you into a good land, a land of brooks of water, of fountains and springs, flowing forth into valleys and hills" (Deut. 8:7). When they had entered into the land, then he said to them: "You have come to the hill country of the Amorites" (1:20), which the Lord your God gives you. And when they said: The time has not yet arrived—[Moses said:] The Lord your God has given you the land. I do not say something as a matter of conjecture or hearsay, rather what you yourself see with your own eyes. "Go up, take possession"—it means, immediately, "as the Lord thy God has said" (v. 21).

[As noted, Sifre on Deuteronomy uses the same parable again, but with important differences: both illustrand and application are different, and instead of "king" there is simply "a man." Here the parable is about the Promised Land, but in the parallel it is concerned with the future life.]

87–88. *The Woman Who Ate Forbidden Figs, The Memorial of a Calamity; perhaps Simeon b. Yohai; ca. 140; Sifre on Deuteronomy 26 (cf. Lev. R. 31:4; Sifre on Num. 137; B. Yoma 86b; Num. R. 19:12)*

"And I besought the Lord at that time" (Deut. 3:23). That is what the verse says: "The poor use entreaties, but the rich answer roughly" (Prov. 18:23). Two good administrators came forth on behalf of Israel—Moses and David the king of Israel. Moses said to the Holy One, blessed be He: Lord of the world, I have committed a sin! May it be specifically written down [in Scripture] that the people may not say: It seems that Moses falsified in the Torah, or that he said something that was not commanded him.

[87] A parable. It is like a king who issued a decree that whoever ate the unripe figs of the seventh year should be publicly displayed and shamed in the hippodrome. Then a woman of good family collected and ate unripe figs of the seventh year, and she was publicly displayed in the hippodrome. Then she said to him: O king, grant that my crime be publicly stated lest the peoples of the king say: It seems that she is being punished for adultery, or perhaps she has been involved in sorcery. But if they see that unripe figs of the

seventh year are hung around my neck, then they will know that it is for this reason that I am punished.

Even so said Moses before the Place (God): May the sin that I committed be written down [in Scripture] against me. The Holy One, blessed be He, said to him: Behold, I write it down that it concerns the water [of Meribah], as it says: "You rebelled against My word in the Wilderness of Sin during the strife of the congregation, to sanctify Me at the waters before their eyes" (Num. 27:14).

[88] R. Simeon says: A parable. It is like a king who was traveling on the road, and his son was with him in his carriage [*carruca*]. He came to a narrow pass, and the carriage overturned on the son. One of his eyes was blinded, a foot was cut off, and a hand was shattered. When the king came again to that same place, he recounted the incident two or three times and said: Here my son suffered a great loss. His eye was blinded; his foot was cut off; his hand was shattered.

So also the Place (God) repeated three times: "The waters of Meribah" (Num. 20:13), "The waters of Meribah" (27:14), "The waters of Meribah" (Deut. 32:51), in order to say: Thus I killed Miriam, thus I killed Aaron, and thus I killed Moses. And so it says: "Their judges were cast down from the rock" (Ps. 141:7).

[In the parallels, no. 87 seems to be attributed to R. Judah b. Ilai, and no. 88 to R. Simeon b. Yohai.]

89. *The Servant Who Was Forbidden Wine; anonymous; Sifre on Deuteronomy 28*

"Let me go over, I pray, and see the good land" (Deut. 3:25). Is it possible that Moses asked of God that he might enter the land? For indeed it had already said: You shall not cross over the Jordan.

A parable. It is like a king who had two servants. He commanded that one of them should not drink wine for thirty days. The latter said: What sort of command is that, that I should not drink wine for thirty days? I could go an entire year, or two years, without drinking wine! Why did he say that? In order to minimize the words of his master. Then the king said that the second servant should not drink wine for thirty days. The latter said: Is it possible that I can live without wine even for an hour? And he said this to indicate the respect that he had for his master's command.

So also Moses demonstrated his respect for the word of God and asked from God that he might still be allowed to enter the land. In this sense it says: "Let me go over, and see."

90. *The Unwise Suitor; R. Simeon b. Yohai; ca. 140; Sifre on Deuteronomy 37*

[Dealing with Moses' description of the Promised Land in Deut. 11:10–15.] R. Simeon b. Yohai said: This one was a fool, for he did not know how to persuade.

A parable. It is like a man who went to court a woman. He said to her: Your father is a king, and I am a king; your father is rich, and I am rich; your father gives you meat and fish to eat and rare wine to drink, and I will give you meat and fish to eat and rare wines to drink. That is no way to persuade. How then? He says to her: Your father is a commoner, but I am a king; your father is poor, but I am rich; your father gives you vegetables and legumes to eat, but I will give you meat and fish to eat; your father gives you new wine to drink, but I will give you rare wine to drink; your father takes you to the baths on foot, but I will take you in a litter [*galgatica*].

Is this not a matter of *qal ve-chomer*? If one came to praise his own land, he surely would not engage in criticism of the land of Israel; *a fortiori* how much more would he rather praise the land of Israel!

[For the term *qal ve-chomer*, see no. 58.]

91. *The King Who Reinforced Obedience; R. Simeon b. Yohai; ca. 140; Sifre on Deuteronomy 40*

[Commenting on Deut. 11:12.]

R. Simeon b. Yohai said: A parable. It is like a king of flesh and blood who had sons and many servants, and they were fed and cared for at his hand. And the key of the storehouse was in his hand. When they did his will, he would open the storehouse, and they would be filled; but

when they did not do his will, he would close the storehouse, and they would nearly die of hunger.

Even so is Israel: when she does the will of God, "The
Lord will give to you His good treasury, the heavens" (Deut.
28:12). But when she does not do the will of God, then will
"the anger of the Lord be kindled against you, and He will
shut up the heavens, so that there will be no rain" (11:17).

92. *The Gluttonous Prince; anonymous; Sifre on Deuteronomy*
    43

If you do this, then will "the anger of the Lord be
kindled against you" (Deut. 11:17).

A parable. It is like a king who sent his son to a banquet;
and he was sitting and charging him and saying to him: My
son, do not eat more than you actually need, and do not
drink more than you actually need in order that you may
return home decently. But the son did not heed this advice.
He ate and he drank more than he needed, and he vomited
and fouled the banquet guests. Then they bundled him by
his hands and his feet and threw him down behind the
palace.

Even so the Holy One, blessed be He, said to them, to
Israel: I brought you into a good and wide land, a land
flowing with milk and honey, to eat its fruit and to be
satisfied with its good things and to bless My name for it.
You did not remain by the good, so now you are under
punishment.

[There is a partial parallel in no. 67.]

93. *The Medicinal Plaster; anonymous; Sifre on Deuteronomy*
    45 (cf. B. Kiddushin 30b.)

"Make these My words into a medicine [reading *śam* for
sam] for your heart" (Deut. 11:18); the Scripture shows that
the words of Torah are like an elixir of life.

A parable. It is like a king who made a great wound on
his son and then placed a plaster on the wound. He said to
him: My son, as long as this plaster is on your wound, eat
and drink whatever you like, and bathe in either warm or

cold water, and you will not be harmed. But if you remove it, you will develop a dangerous ulcer.

Even so the Holy One, blessed be He, spoke to the Israelites: I have created the evil inclination for you, but I have also made the Torah as a medicine for you. As long as you are concerned about the latter, the former will not have power over you; for it says, "If you do well, will you not triumph over him?" (Gen. 4:7). However, if you do not concern yourself with Torah, then it says: "If you do not well, then sin crouches at the door" (ibid.). And not only so, but all your activity will be frustrated, as it says: "And the desire is for you"; but when you will, you can triumph over him: "But you must master it" (ibid.).

[This whole pericope depends upon a wordplay made upon Deut. 11:18. For the doctrine of the evil inclination, see under no. 32.]

94. *The Precious Bird; R. Simeon b. Yohai; ca. 140; Sifre on Deuteronomy 48 (cf. B. Menahoth 99b; ARNa 24:7; ARNb 35*

"For if you will be careful to do all this commandment" (Deut. 11:22). . . . . R. Simeon said: "Only take heed and keep your soul diligently" (4:9).

A parable. It is like a king of flesh and blood who had caught a bird and gave it unto the keeping of his servant. He said to him: Now be careful of this bird, which is for my son. If you lose it, do not imagine that you have lost only a farthing [*assarion*]; rather, it is as though you had lost your own life.

And thus it says: "For it is no trifle for you, but it is your life" (Deut. 32:47).

[An *assarion* (Greco-Latin), or *issar* (Hebrew), was virtually the smallest unit of currency (except for the *perutah*). It is the "farthing" mentioned in Matt. 10:29.]

95. *Two Brothers and Their Earnings; R. Simeon b. Yohai; ca. 140; Sifre on Deuteronomy 48*

"For if you will be careful to do all this commandment" (Deut. 11:22). . . . . Something that you regard as trivial may actually be a matter of life and death.

R. Simeon b. Yohai says: A parable. It is like two brothers who were laying by money behind the back of their father. One would get a dinar and then consume it, and the other would get a dinar and save it. The one who got a dinar and consumed it was found as one who had nothing left in his hand, and the one who got a dinar and saved it was found in later time to be wealthy.

So are the pupils of the sages. If one learns two or three sayings in a day, two or three chapters in a week, two or three sections in a month, then finally he will be found to be a wealthy man, of whom it says: "He who gathers little by little will increase it" (Prov. 13:11). On the other hand, he who says: Today I learn a little, tomorrow I learn a little; today I recite, tomorrow I recite—he will be found as one who has nothing in his hand, and of him it says: "A son who sleeps in harvest brings shame" (10:5); and it says: "The sluggard does not plow in the autumn" (20:4); and it says: "I passed by the field of a sluggard" etc. (24:30).

96. *The Two Paths; anonymous; Sifre on Deuteronomy 53*

"Behold, I set before you this day blessing and curse" (Deut. 11:26). Why is this said, since it says: "I have set before you life and death, blessing and curse" (30:19)? Lest Israel say: Because God set before us two ways, a way of life and a way of death, in which shall we walk? From these passages the teaching is brought out, "And thou shalt choose life" (ibid.).

A parable. It is like one who dwelt by a fork in the road [lit., "a dividing of the ways"]. And there were before him two private paths, one that was smooth at its beginning, but its end was thorny; and one that was thorny at its beginning, but its end was smooth. And he was informing those who passed by and saying to them: You see this path that is smooth at its beginning? For two or three steps you walk in its smoothness, and it ends up in thorns. And you see this other path that is thorny at its beginning? For two or three steps you walk in thorns, but it ends up in smoothness.

Even so Moses said to Israel: You see the wicked when they begin in this world? For two or three days they prosper, but they end up confounded afterward, as it is said, "For the evil man has no future" (Prov. 24:20). . . . You see the righteous who are afflicted in this world? For two or three days they are afflicted, but they end up rejoicing afterward. And thus it says: "That He might humble thee and test thee [to do thee good in the end]" (Deut. 8:16). . . . And it says: "The path of the righteous is like the light of dawn" (Prov. 4:18).

[This is a variation of the "two ways" theme, so common in early Jewish and Christian tradition (cf. 4 Ezra 7:11–14; 1 Enoch 91:4; 2 Enoch 30:15; Testament of Abraham 1:3, 5; etc.), which must ultimately find its source in the Deuteronomic passages cited, if not in Prov. 4:18–19.]

97. The Unsophisticated Dinner Guest; R. Joshua b. Karha; ca. 150; Sifre on Deuteronomy 53

"Behold, I set before you this day a blessing and a curse" (Deut. 11:26). . . .

R. Joshua b. Karha says: A parable. It is like a king who made a banquet and invited the guests. And his dear friend was partaking improperly amid their taunting. And he [the king] was gesturing [to him] how to handle the portion correctly, but he had no understanding.

And thus it says: "I will instruct you and teach you the way you should go; I will counsel you with my eye upon you" (Ps. 32:8).

[This item follows immediately after no. 96. The point is that God gives guidance to those who heed the right way to go.]

98. The Prince Who Was Replaced; R. Nathan the Babylonian; ca. 180; Sifre on Deuteronomy 305

Rabbi Nathan said: Moses was troubled in his heart that none of his sons took his place. Then said the Holy One, blessed be He, to him: Why are you troubled in your heart? The sons of thy brother Aaron are to thee as thy sons, and these, whom I place over Israel, will go and stand at the door of Eleazar.

A parable. Unto what is the matter like? It is like a king

of flesh and blood who had a son, and he was not worthy of taking over the kingship. So he took the kingship away from the son and placed it in the hand of a friend. The king said to him: Since I have given you the power, go, stand before the door of my son.

Even so said the Holy One, blessed be He, to Joshua: Since I have given thee the power, go, stand at the door of Eleazar; as it is said: "And he shall stand before Eleazar the priest" (Num. 27:21).

99. *The Negligent Tutor; anonymous; Sifre on Deuteronomy 306.*

"Give ear, O heavens" (Deut. 32:1).

A parable. It is like a king who handed over his son to a tutor (pedagogue) who was to sit and watch him. The son said: Father assumes that it is important that I be under the care of a tutor. But now I watch him while he eats and drinks and then goes to sleep, and then I go and do whatever I wish and desire. His father said to him: The problem is not that I handed you over to the tutor, but that he was negligent and was allowing you to stray.

Even so, Moses said to the Israelites: Lest you think to flee from under the wings of the Shekinah or to depart from the earth and not return: these are written about the heavens, as it is said: "The heavens will reveal his iniquity" (Job. 20:27); and in the same writings it is proved that also the earth knows, as it is said: "And the earth will rise up against him" (ibid.).

["Tutor" is an inadequate translation of *piydagog/paidagōgos* (see no. 74), but English does not provide a better equivalent. The ancient "pedagogue" was not an instructor in the modern sense but rather something like a male nanny, a servant who accompanied his wealthy young charge to school and elsewhere in order to monitor the boy's behavior.]

100. *The Intractable Rod; anonymous; Sifre on Deuteronomy*
    308

"A generation perverse and perverted" (Deut. 32:5).
Moses said to the Israelites: You are twisted, you are
perverted, you belong to the fire.

Unto what is the matter like? It is like one who has a
crooked rod in his hand that he turns over to a workman to
straighten. If it does not straighten out, then he tries to
straighten it with a roller. If it still does not become straight,
he pounds it with a hammer and thrusts it into the fire.

And thus it says: "And I will deliver you into the hand
of brutal men, forgers [or, smiths] of destruction" (Ezek.
21:31).

101. *The Unworthy Tenants; anonymous; Sifre on*
    Deuteronomy 312

"For the Lord's portion is His people" (Deut. 32:9).

A parable. It is like a king who owned a field and who
gave it over to renters. They took it but robbed the owner.
Then he took it away from them and gave it to their children,
but they turned out to be even worse than the others. Then a
son was born to the king, and he said to them: Get out of my
possession. You can no longer remain there; give me back
my portion.

Even so when our father Abraham was alive, he brought
forth evil: Ishmael and the sons of Keturah. Then when our
father Isaac was alive, he brought forth evil: Esau, the ruler
of Edom, who was even worse than the others. But when
Jacob was alive, he did not bring forth evil, but all his sons
were honest, as he himself was. Whom did God call his
portion? Was it not Jacob, for it says: "And Jacob was a quiet
man, dwelling in tents" (Gen. 25:27). Wherefore God
obtained His portion from Jacob, as it is said: "The Lord's
portion is His people, and Jacob His allotted heritage" (Deut.
32:9); and it says: "For the Lord has chosen Jacob for
Himself" (Ps. 135:4).

102. *The Brave Hero; anonymous; Sifre on Deuteronomy 313*

"He found him in a desert land" (Deut. 32:10). That is Abraham.

A parable. It is like a king who went out, he and his army, to the desert. His army forsook him in a place of hostility, in a place of enemy troops, in a place of robbers. And a certain brave man went to him and said to him: My lord and king, Do not allow your heart to fail, and have no anxiety. By your life, I swear that I will not desert you until you are back in your palace and asleep in your own bed.

Accordingly it says: "And He said unto him: I am the Lord who brought you up from the Chaldees" (Gen. 15:7). . . .

[In this parable the king represents Abraham, while God is represented by a brave man (*gibor*), a reversal of tropes that has scarcely any parallels.]

103. *The Wise Advocate; anonymous; Sifre on Deuteronomy 343*

"He said: The Lord came from Sinai and dawned from Seir" (Deut. 33:2). The Scripture is speaking of when Moses opened (his discourse). He did not begin with the problem of Israel until he opened his speech with praise for God [*ha-Maqom*, "the Place").

A parable. It is like an orator who was standing upon the podium [*bema*], and it was advantageous to refrain from the case at hand and not begin with the problem of the client ['*ish*] until he opened his speech with the praise of the king: "Happy is the realm whose king he is. Happy is the realm whose judge he is. Over us shines the sun, over us shines the moon." Then all joined in this acclamation for the king. Afterward the orator began with the presentation of his case for the man. At the end he concluded again with the king's praises.

Also our teacher Moses did not begin to speak about the problem of Israel until he had introduced the praise of God, for it says: "The Lord came from Sinai" (Deut. 33:2). Then he began to deal with the question of Israel's need, for it says:

"Thus the Lord was king in Jeshurun" (v. 5). And then at the end he concluded with the praise of the Lord: "There is none like God, O Jeshurun" (v. 26).

104. *The Repatriated Prince; anonymous; Sifre on Deuteronomy 345 (cf. Exod. R. 33:7)*

"A possession of the assembly of Jacob" (Deut. 33:4). . . . The word *possession* teaches that the Torah is a possession of Israel.

A parable. Unto what is the matter like? It is like a son of kings who, as a child, was taken captive into a distant province. If he is summoned, even though it be after a hundred years, he is not ashamed to return and face it, for he says: I am returning to my own possession.

Even so, a wise scholar who separated from the words of Torah and then afterward walked according to them, if he is summoned to return, even though it be after a hundred years, he is not ashamed to return and face it, for he says: I am returning to my own possession. It is as it is said: "A possession of the assembly of Jacob" (Deut. 33:4).

[The application attached to this parable seems to have in view cases like that of the apostate R. Elisha b. Abuyah (cf. Ruth R. 6:4), but it may be an example of reapplication, for the most natural application would be to Israel's return from captivity.]

105. *The Favored Son; anonymous; Sifre on Deuteronomy 352*

Why was Benjamin honored so that the Shekinah dwelt in his portion?

A parable. It is like a king who on occasion visited his sons. Each one of them said: He will live with me. The youngest son said: Is it possible that my father will leave the others and live with me? He went and stood with sad countenance while his spirit was depressed. His father saw him standing there with sad countenance while his spirit was depressed. He said: Have you noticed how my youngest son stands there with sad countenance while his spirit is depressed? Now my food and drink will come from you [the other brothers], but my dwelling place will be with him [the youngest son].

Even so the Holy One, blessed be He, said: The house of My choice will be in the portion of Benjamin, and the offerings will come from all the tribes.

106. *The Wise and Foolish Depositaries; anonymous; Sifre on Deuteronomy 357*

When God takes the souls of the righteous, He takes them away with the spirit of peace.

They parable a parable. Unto what is the matter like? It is like a trusted man in a city, to whom all came to leave deposits [for safekeeping]. Then when one came to collect [his own], he brought it out and returned it to him, for he knew exactly where it was to be found. But when he left the responsibility to his son or his slave or his delegate, then everything was turned upside down because they did not know where each was.

Even so when God takes away the souls of the righteous, He does so with the spirit of peace. But when He takes away the souls of the wicked, He turns them over to the grim and terrifying angels that they may wrench away their souls. Thus it says: "A cruel messenger will be sent against him" (Prov. 17:11); and it says: "They die through the shaking out of their souls" (variant on Job 36:14).

GENESIS RABBAH

The Midrash Rabbah is a collection of ten midrashim of various dates. In a sense, the series is the creation of publishers, each document being quite independent of the others. Genesis (or Bereshith) Rabbah is the oldest component of the series, which is comprised of midrashim for the five books of the Pentateuch and the five Megilloth (Scrolls) read at festivals. Genesis Rabbah is a Palestinian work, its redaction being virtually completed not long after that of the Palestinian Talmud in the early fifth century C.E., though there are later additions to the last part of the work. Out of some sixteen items we present here six.

107–8. *The Throne and the Footstool, The Nether and Upper Portions of a Palace; Beth Shammai and Beth Hillel; ca. 60; Gen. R. 1:15 (cf. Lev. R. 36:1; P. Hagigah 2:1)*

"The heaven and the earth" (Gen. 1:1). Beth [or, "the School of"] Shammai maintain: The heaven was created first; while Beth Hillel hold: The earth was created first.

[107] Beth Shammai: A parable. It is like a king who first made his throne and then his footstool.

Even so said the Holy One, blessed be He: "The heaven is My throne, and the earth is My footstool" (Isa. 66:1).

[108] Beth Hillel: A parable. It is like a king who builds a palace; after building the nether portion, he builds the upper.

Even so, it is written: "In the day that the Lord God made earth and heaven" (Gen. 2:4).

[If this attribution is correct, these may be the earliest rabbinic true parables. The rival schools of Shammai and Hillel belong to the first generation of Tannaim, traditionally dated from 10 to 80 C.E.]

109. *The Villager Who Smashed Glassware; R. Johanan b. Zakkai, ca. 80; or R. Akiba, ca. 130; Gen. R. 19:6*

"And the eyes of them both were opened" (Gen. 3:7). Were they then blind?

R. Judan in the name of R. Johanan b. Zakkai, or R. Berekiah in the name of R. Akiba, said: A parable. It is like a villager who was passing by a glassworker's shop, and just when a basket full of goblets and cut glassware was in front of him, he swung his staff round and broke them. And he [the proprietor] arose and seized him and said to him: I know that I cannot obtain redress from you, but come and I will show you how much valuable stuff you have destroyed.

Even so He showed them how many generations they had destroyed.

110. *The Dying Athlete; R. Simeon b. Yohai; ca. 140; Gen. R. 22:9*

[Commenting on Gen. 4:10, "The voice of thy brother's blood crieth out unto Me from the ground."] R. Simeon b. Yohai said: It is difficult to say this thing, and the mouth cannot utter it plainly.

It is like two athletes who wrestled before the king; had the king wished, he could have separated them. But he did not so desire, and one overcame the other and killed him, he crying out (before he died): Let my cause be pleaded before the king!

Even so, "The voice of thy brother's blood crieth out *against* Me" [reading *'alay* instead of *'elay*].

111. *The Pearl Lost and Found; R. Nehemiah; ca. 150; Gen. R. 39:10 (cf. Ruth R. 8:1)*

[Discussing the selection of Abraham.]

R. Berekiah b. R. Simon said in the name of R. Nehemiah: It is like a king who was passing from place to place, and a gem fell from his head. And the king halted and stationed his retinue there, gathered the sand in piles, and brought sieves. He sifted the first pile but did not find it; the second but did not find it; but in the third he found it. They said: The king has found his pearl.

Even so, the Holy One, blessed be He, said to Abraham: What need had I to trace the descent of Shem, Arpachshad, Shelah, Eber, Peleg, Reu, Serug, Nahor, and Terah? Was it not on thy account? Thus it is written, "And foundest his [Abraham's] heart faithful before Thee" (Neh. 9:8).

112. *The Hero Only in His Mother's Eyes; R. Eleazar b. Simon; ca. 180; Gen. R. 65:11 (cf. Song R. 2:15:2)*

"He called Esau his elder son" (Gen. 27:1).

R. Leazar b. R. Simon said: It is like a province that was levying a bodyguard for the king. Now a certain woman there had a son, a dwarf, whom she used to call Tallswift.

She said: My son is tall and swift; why then do you not appoint him? They said to her: If in your eyes he is tall and swift, in ours he is but a dwarf.

Even so, his [Esau's] father called him great: "He called Esau his great [*gadol*] son" (Gen. 27:1); his mother too called him great: "And Rebekah took the choicest garments of Esau her great son" (v. 15). Said the Holy One, blessed be He, to them: If in your eyes he is great, in Mine he is small; as it says: "Behold, I make thee small among the nations" (Obad. 1:2).

[R. Eleazar was the son of R. Simeon (often shortened to Simon) b. Yohai. In the parallel this parable is incorrectly attributed to "Simon b. Eleazar." Eleazar was often shortened to Leazar or Lazar ("Lazarus" in the New Testament).]

LEVITICUS RABBAH

After Genesis Rabbah, Leviticus is the next oldest part of the Midrash Rabbah, redacted between the beginning of the fifth and the seventh centuries. As is the case with all rabbinic literature, the traditions from which it is compiled are of course generally much older. Out of sixteen items we present only one.

113. *The Foolish Shipmate; R. Simeon b. Yohai; ca. 140; Lev. R. 4:6*

It is said, "Shall one man sin, and wilt Thou be wroth with all the congregation?" (Num. 16:22).

R. Simeon b. Yohai taught: A parable. It is like men who were sitting in a ship. One took a drill and began boring beneath his own place. His fellow travelers said to him: What are you doing? He said to them: What does that matter to you? Am I not drilling under my own place? They said: Because the water will come up and flood the ship for us all.

Even so did Job say: "And be it indeed that I have erred, mine error remaineth with myself" (Job 19:4); and his friends said: "He adds transgression unto his sin; he extends it among us." (a questionable translation of Job 34:37) [They said to him:] You extend your sins among us.

[This pericope is preceded by the general point that the

many may suffer because of one, expressed in a way quite reminiscent of 1 Cor. 12:26.]

DEUTERONOMY RABBAH

Deuteronomy (or Debarim) Rabbah is relatively late, compiled about the ninth or tenth century. Out of six items we present one.

114. *The Errant Son; R. Meir; ca. 150; Deut. R. 2:24*

Another explanation: "Thou wilt return to the Lord thy God" (Deut. 4:30).

R. Samuel Pargrita said in the name of R. Meir: Unto what is the matter like? It is like the son of a king who took to evil ways. The king sent a tutor to him who appealed to him, saying: Repent, my son. But the son sent him back to his father [with a message], How can I have the effrontery to return? I am ashamed to come before you. Thereupon his father sent back word: My son, is a son ever ashamed to return to his father? And is it not to your father that you will be returning?

Even so the Holy One, blessed be He, sent Jeremiah to Israel when they sinned, and said to him: Go, say to my children: Return. Whence this? For it is said: "Go and proclaim these words" etc. (Jer. 3:12). Israel asked Jeremiah: How can we have the effrontery to return to God? Whence do we know this? For it is said: "Let us lie down in our shame and let our confusion cover us" etc. (v. 25). But God sent back word to them: My children, if you return, will you not be returning to your Father? Whence this? "For I am become a father to Israel" etc. (Jer. 31:9).

[The similarity of this parable both to no. 104 and to the gospel parable of the Prodigal Son (Luke 15:11–32) is striking.]

SONG OF SONGS RABBAH

Song of Songs (or Shir ha-Shirim) Rabbah expounds that book of the Bible allegorically as a description of the relation between God and Israel. It draws from earlier midrashim and from the Palestinian Talmud, and it has been dated between 600 and 750 C.E. Out of twelve items we present one.

115. *The Lost Coin; R. Phineas b. Jair; ca. 200; Song R. 1:1:9*

R. Phineas b. Jair opened his exposition with the text "If thou seek her as silver" etc. (Prov. 2:4). If you seek after words of Torah as after hidden treasures, the Holy One, blessed be He, will not withhold your reward.

A parable. It is like a man [who] if he loses a *sela* [half a shekel] or an *obol* in his house, he lights lamp after lamp, wick after wick, until he finds it.

But behold, if for these things that are only ephemeral and of this world a man will light so many lamps and lights till he finds where they are hidden, how much more ought you to search for the words of the Torah, which are the life both of this world and of the next world, as for hidden treasure? Hence, "If thou seek her as silver" etc.

[The two coins mentioned were moderately valuable units of currency.]

APPENDIX TO PART 1

Many items in the rabbinic literature do not conform fully to the genre of parable as we define it in part 2, but many of these items are of considerable interest on other grounds, and some of them are closely related to the parable form. We provide ten of these items in this appendix (distinguished here with an *A* prefix). We have arranged them under classifications that are briefly explained, but we provide the same information about each item that we have presented for the regular parables in part 1, including the source from which each is taken. Three of the items come from sources that were not described earlier, namely: Ecclesiastes Rabbah, a component of the Midrash Rabbah that may be dated without certainty to the seventh century C.E.; Pesikta Rabbati, a homiletic midrash of Palestinian origin, likewise of uncertain date, but sometimes placed in the seventh century C.E.; and Pirqe de R. Eliezer, a very unusual midrash pseudepigraphically attributed to one of the early Tannaim and containing much early material but probably put together in the eighth or ninth century C.E.

Example Stories

In the rabbinic literature there are semianecdotal stories designed to illustrate a positive or negative duty and concluding with an admonition. They are never called *meshalim*, the word used for parables, but are rather termed *me'asim*, the word also used for anecdotes. In the gospel of Luke such stories are called parables (e.g., the Good Samaritan, Luke 10:25–37), but technically we distinguish them from regular parables and call them example stories.

A1. *The Poor Widow and Her Two Sons; perhaps R. Josiah; ca. 180; ARNa 38*

"Pestilence comes upon the world" (E.g., Lev. 19:9–10 combined with Lev. 26:25) for neglect of the [laws about] the harvest gleanings, the forgotten sheaf, the corner of the field, and the poor man's tithe.

There was once a (poor) woman who dwelt in the neighborhood of a landowner. Her two sons went out to gather gleanings, but the landowner did not let them take any. Their mother kept saying: When will my sons come back from the field? Perhaps I shall find that they have brought something to eat. And they kept saying: When shall we go back to our mother? Perhaps we shall discover that she has found something to eat. But she found that they had nothing, and they found that she had nothing to eat. So they laid their heads on their mother's lap, and the three of them died in one day.

Said the Holy One, blessed be He: Their very existence you take away from them! By your life! I shall make you, too, pay for it with your very existence!

[The law of Moses prescribed that at harvest time the gleanings be left for the poor (Lev. 19:9–10; 23:22; Deut. 24:19–21). A whole tractate of the Mishnah (Peah) is devoted to this law.]

A2. *The Woman Who Swore Rashly; R. Haggai (a later rabbi); P. Shebuoth 6:5 (cf. Lev. R. 6:3; Pesikta Rabbati 22:6)*

The stones that fire does not consume will be annihilated as a consequence of false oaths. R. Jonah said: (It will be thus only) for false oaths sworn deceitfully. R. Jose says: (It will be thus) also for false oaths sworn in good faith. Haggai interprets according to the opinion of R. Jose.

A woman went to her neighbor's house to knead some dough, having in her purse two denarii. These fell into the dough and were baked into the bread. She discovered that the money was missing and went home to search, but she did not find it. She returned to her neighbor's and said to her: Give me my two denarii that fell out in your house. The neighbor said: I swear I know nothing about it. If I know, may my son be buried! And her son was buried. Returning from the cemetery, she heard people saying: If the matter had been as she said, she would not have had to bury her son. Whereupon she repeated her oath, and another son died. When people came to console her and they broke the bread for the funeral meal, the two denarii fell out of one loaf.

The affair teaches: Whether you are innocent or guilty, do not lightly make an oath.

Vertical Comparisons

A number of rabbinic *meshalim* (the plural of *mashal*, "parable") use the expressions "a king of flesh and blood" or "according to the custom of the world" to introduce terrestrial behavior that is then compared with God's behavior. Many of these items lack the usual introductory formulas that identify parables, and most of them depict a general situation rather than narrate a specific event. We have thought it best not to include such similitudes, in contrast to parables such as nos. 94 and 98, among the regular parables. We may call them vertical comparisons, though most of them contrast human and divine characteristics, while a few stress the parallels.

A3. *Royal Decrees; R. Eliezer b. Hyrcanus; ca. 80; P. Rosh Hashanah 1:3 (cf. Lev. R. 35:3)*

R. Eliezer said: *Para basileos ho nomos agraphos* [a Greek proverb meaning, "For a king the law is unwritten"—a king may disregard his own law].

In the custom of the world, a king of flesh and blood issues a decree and performs it or has others perform it as he pleases.

But the Holy One, blessed be He, is not so. He issued a decree and performed it in the beginning, as it is said in Leviticus 22:9, "They shall keep My decree. . . . I am the Lord"; that is to say, I am He who kept the commandments of the Torah in the beginning.

A4. *A King in Festival and at War; R. Judah ha-Nasi; ca. 200; Pesikta Rabbati 21:9 (cf. Midrash on Ps. 18:17)*

[Commenting on Ps. 18:13.]
R. Judah II the Patriarch said: In the custom of the world when a king of flesh and blood goes on a May festival, he goes with some ten men; but when he goes to war, he goes forth with companies and with legions.

But the Holy One, blessed be He, does not act thus. When He revealed Himself at the Red Sea to wage war for His sons, He appeared to them by Himself: "The Lord is a man of war" (Exod. 15:3); but when He came down on Mount Sinai to give Torah to Israel, Michael and his retinue came down with Him, Gabriel and his retinue: "And the Lord my God shall come, and all His holy ones with Him" (Zech. 14:5).

[There is some similarity between this item and parable no. 50.]

Fables

The Rabbis made use of the fables from Indian and Greek sources. In fact, as the Introduction points out, some Rabbis were famous for their repertoire of fox fables. Sometimes these fables are introduced with the standard formulas of regular parables, and we have therefore felt justified in including them as such (e.g., no. 18). But perhaps more often these resident aliens have been put to work without being circumcised.

A5. *The Fox That Offered to Appease the Lion; R. Levi; ca. 300; Gen. R. 78:7*

[Illustrating Gen. 33:1.]

R. Levi said: A lion was angry with the cattle and the beasts. Said they: Who will go to appease him? Said the fox: I know three hundred fables, and I will appease him. They said: Let it be so. He went a short distance and halted. They asked: Why have you halted? He answered: I have forgotten a hundred. They replied: In two hundred there are blessings. He went on a little and again halted. They said: What does this mean? He said: I have forgotten another hundred. They replied: Even a hundred will do. When he arrived there, he said: I have forgotten them all, so everyone must appease for himself.

So it was with Jacob. R. Judah b. Simon said: [Jacob declared]: I have the strength to engage in prayer [against him]; R. Levi said: [Jacob declared]: I have strength to wage a battle. But when he arrived there, "then he divided the children" etc. (Gen. 33:1), saying to them: Let the merit of each one protect him.

A6. *The Fox That Fasted, Feasted, and Fasted; Geniba; ca. 260; Eccl. R. 5:14:1*

"As he came forth from his mother's womb" (Eccl. 5:15).

It is like a fox who found a vineyard that was fenced in on all sides. There was one hole through which he wanted to enter, but he was unable to do so. What did he do? He fasted for three days until he became lean and frail, and so got in through the hole. Then he ate and became fat again, so that when he wished to go out, he could not pass through at all. He again fasted another three days until he became lean and frail, returning to his former condition, and went out. When he was outside, he turned his face and, gazing at the vineyard, said: O vineyard, O vineyard, how good are you and the fruits inside! All that is beautiful and commendable, but what enjoyment has one from you? As one enters you, so he comes out.

Such is this world.

[This item has been given the form of a regular parable, but since it comes from a Rabbi later than the Tannaitic period, we have included it in the appendix because of its intrinsic interest.]

Miscellaneous Fringe Items

We conclude this appendix with some items left out of our corpus of regular parables for various reasons but still particularly interesting. Some of them are quite early, but not typical parables. Others are couched in the formulas of regular parables, though they are really nothing more than a simple metaphor or simile, or perhaps a series of metaphors and similes.

A7. *The Exact Accounting; R. Akiba; ca. 130; M. Aboth 3:17*

All is given against a pledge, and the net is cast over all living; the shop stands open and the shopkeeper gives credit and the account book lies open and the hand writes and everyone that wishes to borrow let him come and borrow; but the collectors go their rounds continually every day and exact payment of men with their consent or without their consent, for they have that on which they can rely; and the judgment is a judgment of truth; and all is made ready for the banquet.

[This item occurs in a list of sayings attributed to Akiba. The traditional interpretation is: From the day of one's birth, all that he has is on loan from God; no one can escape the net of the angel of death and the Day of Judgment; the ways of good and evil are opened up to men, and an account is kept of their actions; the collectors are the angels of death; and the banquet is the life of the world to come.]

A8. The Audience with a King; Hillel; before 10 C.E.; ARNa 15:3 (cf. ARNb 29)

Once a Gentile was passing behind a synagogue, and he heard a child reciting the verse, "And these are the garments that they shall make: a breastplate and an ephod and a robe" (Exod. 28:4). He came to Shammai and said to him: Master, for whom is all that finery? He said: For the High Priest who stands and ministers at the altar. The Gentile said to him: Make me a proselyte on condition that you appoint me High Priest. Shammai said: Is there no priest in Israel, and have we no High Priests in Israel to serve in the high priesthood, except this insignificant proselyte who comes with staff and script only and wishes to minister as High Priest? He rebuked him and angrily drove him away. The Gentile then came to Hillel and said to him: Master make me a proselyte on condition that you appoint me High Priest, so that I may stand and minister at the altar.

Hillel said to him: Sit down, and I will tell thee something. One who wishes to have an audience before a king of flesh and blood, is it not right that he learn how to make his entrances and exits?

He said to him: Yes.

Thou wishest to have an audience before the King of kings, the Holy One, blessed be He. Is it not all the more right that thou learn how to enter into the Holy of Holies, how to fix the lights, how to approach the altar, how to set the table, how to prepare the row of wood?

He said to him: Do what is good in thine eyes.

[Other quasi-parabolic metaphors are attributed to Hillel in Lev. R. 34:3.]

A9. The Craftsman and His Tools; R. Johanan b. Zakkai; ca. 80; ARNa 22:1

[Commenting on M. Aboth 3:10.]

They asked Rabban Johanan b. Zakkai: One who is wise and fears sin, what is he? He said to them: Behold, he is a craftsman who has the tools of his craft in his hand.

One who is wise but does not fear sin, what is he? He

said to them: Behold he is a craftsman who has not the tools of his craft in his hand.

One who fears sin but is not wise, what is he? He said to them: Behold, he is no craftsman, but the tools of his craft are in his hand.

A10. *The Robing of Seeds; supposedly R. Eliezer b. Hyrcanus; ca. 90; Pirqe de R. Eliezer 33 (cf. B. Sanhedrin 90b)*

R. Eliezer said: All the dead will arise at the resurrection of the dead, dressed in their shrouds. Know thou that this is the case.

Come thou and learn from the one seeding the earth. He plants naked (seeds), and they arise covered with many coverings.

And the people who descend into the earth dressed, will they not rise up dressed?

[The parallel is ascribed to R. Meir, who is pictured answering a question from Queen Cleopatra: When the dead arise, shall they arise nude or in their garments?]

Part 2

ESSAYS

1

INITIAL QUESTIONS

Often the most elementary questions are the hardest to answer, and so it is with the subject of this book. What, indeed, is a parable? To whom should parables be attributed? And when did the use of parables as a teaching device emerge?

WHEN IS A "PARABLE" A PARABLE?

Definitions can be as tricky as they are crucial. When pressed, we sometimes can do no better than admit, "I can't define it, but I know one when I see one!"

Most readers of the New Testament thought they knew what a parable was until the German scholar Adolf Jülicher published his epoch-making two-volume study *Die Gleichnisreden Jesu* (1886, 1899). Drawing his definitions from Aristotle's *Rhetoric*, Jülicher contended that there is a sharp contrast between parable and allegory. For him, an allegory is an extended metaphor that must be decoded in order to be understood, whereas a parable is an extended simile that makes a transparently simple comparison. Both kinds of trope can be divided into an "illustration half" (*Bildhälfte*) and an "actuality half" (*Sachhälfte*). In the case of allegories there are many points of comparison (*tertia comparationis*) between the two aspects of the trope, but in the case of a true parable there is only one *tertium comparationis*. That is to say, in an allegory every detail means something, but in a real parable there is only one point, and the rest of the story is merely stage machinery necessary to make a credible story. Furthermore, Jülicher insisted that there is no such thing as a mixture of the two kinds of figure. "Half allegory and half parable," he said, "are just mythological beings."

This sharp distinction was important for the interpretation of the parables of Jesus. Jülicher was reacting against what he perceived as the prevailing tendency ever since the time of the early church fathers to interpret the gospel parables as though they were allegories. A very famous example is Augustine's explanation of the story of the Good Samaritan (*Quaestionum Evangeliorum* 2.19), in which he taught that the man who went down from Jerusalem to Jericho represents Adam and the whole human race, who fell from the heavenly city into mortality; the thieves are the Devil and his angels; the wounds are sins; and so on. Every feature of the story means something else; everything in the story is a point of comparison with the theological actuality that it encodes. Against this interpretation Jülicher vigorously protested: the parables of Jesus were true parables, not allegories.

One difficulty here was that in the Gospels themselves, some of the parables are interpreted as though they are allegories, in Jülicher's sense of the terms. Thus in Matthew 13 the Parable of the Sower and the Parable of the Net are each explained in such a way that each salient feature of these stories has a specific meaning. So Jülicher concluded that the interpretations we sometimes see in the Gospels attached to the parables of Jesus are unauthentic: they are not original meanings intended by Jesus but rather were devised by the early church. Jesus told true parables, not allegories, said Jülicher, who devoted the second volume of his work to reconstructing the original meanings.

We cannot here describe further the history of the discussion that Jülicher's work initiated. We have referred to his work only to demonstrate that both the rationale and the results of deciding what constitutes a parable can be quite crucial.

There are two opposite ways to approach the definition of parable in a literary corpus such as the New Testament or the rabbinic literature. One way is the *normative,* or deductive, approach, which sets up an a priori definition on the basis of form, content, function, or all three and dismisses anything that does not fit into that predetermined definition. Jülicher took such an approach. The other way is the *descriptive,* or inductive, approach, which seeks to base a definition on generalizations derived from the analysis of concrete specimens.

In practice, both approaches are forced to make compromises. The normative approach is likely to find few if any specimens in real life that fit perfectly into categories too strictly defined, and so it begins to speak of modified or mixed forms in relating the specimens to its rather artificial categories. The inductive approach, however, finds itself in a vicious circle, for before it can manufacture a description of the specimens it has selected, it must first select the specimens on the basis of a preliminary criterion. It is easy to define a bird as a vertebrate that flies if we base that generalization only on a collection of specimens, however large, that was chosen by looking only for specimens that are vertebrates and that fly. Granted that we should base our concept of the nature of parables on an examination of the things themselves, our selection of what things we shall examine already implies some preconception.

The normative-deductive approach has advantages. It supplies a clear starting point for selection. It makes generic distinctions clear. It is convenient. It has universality: its categories can be applied to (or imposed upon) any corpus of literature, thus making easy comparisons between corpora. But this approach also has serious disadvantages. It suffers from artificiality and overprecision, so that there is difficulty in applying it to real data—the category is narrower than the species being categorized. Its irrelevance to form-critical and historical questions is too easily overlooked, so that there is a temptation to draw such conclusions on the basis of an artificial definition. And this approach also falls into the pitfall of circularity: a parable is such and such; everything that is not such and such cannot be a parable—which begs the question.

The descriptive-inductive approach has advantages. Since it is inductive, there is no problem in squaring its categories with live specimens. It puts historical and form-critical conclusions on a more legitimate basis. It avoids, at least in theory, a priori judgments. But it also has disadvantages. It must have some assumptions in order to make a beginning: there must be a principle of selection. Categorical arbitrariness can never be perfectly eliminated without making the universal coterminous with the individual item, which is to deny the validity of all meaningful classification. And since the descriptive approach seeks to derive its categories only from the corpus at hand, not imposing an alien system (as Jülicher did by forcing the New Testament into Aristotelian rhetorical categories), it makes comparisons between corpora (e.g., between rabbinic literature and the New Testament) far more difficult, or possible only to the extent that the corpora can be considered genetically or generically related.

Our problem in either case is breaking out of the circularity. We must decide what parables are before we can collect them; but we must analyze a collection before we can generalize about what one is.

Using the most nearly objective criterion we can find, we shall take as our starting point the position of Raymond Pautrel in "Les canons du Mashal rabbinique," *Recherches de science religieuse* 26 (1936): 8–9. Beginning with the rabbinic word for parable(s), *mashal/meshalim*, we shall consider to be a parable everything that the ancient Rabbis so designated with this word. But while that is a good place to start, the matter is more complicated. As Pautrel recognized, the Rabbis did not attach the label *mashal* to every specimen, even though there are many items that possess all the same marks and characteristics as those explicitly so labeled. Even more important, the term covers a very wide range of meanings and genres that by modern analysis appear distinct. The rabbinic *mashal* and the New Testament *parabolē* largely cover the same semantic area but are not perfectly identical. The Greek *parabolē* seems to cover a somewhat more restricted range of genres, but in one case may extend over a domain not covered by *mashal* (the example story, which we explain below).

Our policy will therefore be to select as *meshalim* items that are designated as such by introductory formulas *and* items whose structure is identical with these but lack explicit labeling as such. That is our principle of inclusion. In order to make our project manageable, however, we must add a principle of exclusion: we shall concentrate only on narrative *meshalim* that describe a past or typical event, leaving out short word-pictures that are clearly nothing more than simple similes or metaphors, as well as proverbs and riddles, even though all of these forms are called *meshalim* in the rabbinic literature.

Certain elements clearly mark a literary item as a narrative *mashal*. The presence of any one of these marks qualifies an item for inclusion.

Explicit label. Often the introductory formulas to the items explicitly label them as *meshalim*. Some typical introductions are: "A parable"; "A parable: It is like unto . . ."; and "They parable a parable. Unto what is the matter like? It is like unto. . . ."

Abbreviated label. Frequently the introductory formulas are abbreviated in such a way that the word *mashal* itself is omitted: "It is like unto. . . ."

Structural characteristics. The immediate environment and internal structure of the typical narrative *mashal* in its fullest form include these five parts:

1. Illustrand, or the point to be illustrated.
2. Introductory formula, such as noted above.
3. The parable proper (the so-called picture half, or story part, of the whole unit).
4. Application, usually introduced by the Hebrew word *kak* (even so; likewise) or another linking word.
5. Scriptural quotation, often introduced by the formula "as it is said" or "as it is written." (The quotation is often followed by a second application, which itself may become an illustrand, thus producing a chain of parables.)

The full structural pattern just described is both typical and common, but frequently one or more of these elements is lacking. While only the third element (the parable proper) is indispensable, in fact all specimens have at least one of the other elements. All these components will be discussed in the subsequent essays.

We have not included function as a decisive criterion, for form appears to be a more nearly objective characteristic to use. In a general way, all narrative *meshalim* function in their contexts to illustrate or to prove, but we do not include all items that illustrate or prove among the number of narrative

18774

meshalim, for that purpose can be served by other items that are morphologically and structurally quite different.

To make clearer where we have drawn the boundaries, we here list several items that fall outside our consideration. We recognize, of course, that certain specific items share some features of parables as we define them.

Byword. Among the carryovers from the Old Testament meaning of *mashal* is its use in describing a person or people. In B. Baba Bathra 15a, for example, Job is regarded as a human *mashal* (= "type"?) rather than a historical personage.

Proverb. Proverbs and folk sayings are also bearers of the rabbinic term *mashal*, such as the one cited by R. Levi in Song R. 1:2:3: "One who has been bitten by a snake is afraid of a rope."

Parabolic act or other *object lesson* that the Rabbis employed to make their point.

Simile. The dividing line between simple simile and parable can become especially thin, perhaps only a matter of length. C. H. Dodd distinguished between them on the basis of how many verbs the item has.

Metaphor. The distinction between metaphor and allegory is again mainly one of length. The difference between these and simile or parable is mainly that the comparison is formally less explicit, as will be seen. Cf. nos. A7 and A9 in part 1.

Fable. Stories in which animals talk like people and that teach some moral or prudential lesson are associated with the name of Aesop, but ultimately they can be traced back to Indian and ancient Near Eastern origins. The Rabbis became especially fond of fox fables, and sometimes they dressed them up as regular parables by giving them the forms noted above. For examples of pure fable, see nos. A5 and A6. Akiba's story of the Fox and the Fishes (no. 18) is a fable that has been dressed up as a rabbinic parable.

Anecdote. These are stories purported to be about named historic individuals.

Example story. For both anecdotes and example stories Hebrew used the term *ma'eseh* (plural, *me'asim*), but unlike most anecdotes, example stories usually do not name the persons involved. They illustrate a positive or negative duty and conclude with an admonition, which may be moral or prudential. The admonitions that conclude example stories are expressed typically in the imperative mode, in contrast to the applications of parables, which are formally in the indicative. See nos. A1 and A2. In the gospel of Luke several of the stories identified or traditionally known as parables are really example stories: the Good Samaritan (10:25–37), the Rich Fool (12:16–21), the Rich Man and Lazarus (16:19–31), and the Pharisee and the Publican (18:9–14).

Analogy. No. A10 is an example of an argument by analogy.

Vertical comparison. Very frequently the Rabbis compared the ways of God with those of kings or other persons "of flesh and blood," or contrasted the ways of heaven with "the custom of the world." Sometimes these comparisons are explicitly labeled *mashal,* but we have decided to give only two examples, in the appendix (nos. A3 and A4).

TO WHOM SHOULD PARABLES BE ATTRIBUTED?

Roughly one-third of the parables in the present collection are anonymous, while two-thirds appear to be attributed to specific Rabbis or to groups such as the School of Hillel, the School of Shammai, or the School of Ishmael. But the present collection provides an inadequate estimate of the percentage of anonymous parables in the general corpus of rabbinic literature. Since the attempt has been made here to illustrate early rabbinic usage, anonymous parables have been included only from the rabbinic literature that is predominantly Tannaitic (Mishnah, Tosefta, Mekilta, Sifra, and Sifre). From the later literature parables have been included only if attributed to Tannaitic Rabbis (except in the appendix, where this principle is ignored). By not including anonymous parables from the later literature, we have artificially increased the proportion of parables with specific attribution. It is likely that in the total corpus something like half of the parables are anonymous.

But the question of the authorship of individual parables is complex even when they appear to be attributed to specific authors. We must ask, How explicit is the attribution? And then, Is the attribution correct? In some cases the attribution of a parable to a specific Rabbi is so explicit that no problem arises about the intention of the writer. See, for example, nos. 41–42 and 44. On the other hand, there are numerous instances in which a Rabbi is identified as the author of a statement, and then a parable is attached to that statement by way of amplification. Did the writer intend to attribute the parable to the previously named Rabbi, or is the reader expected to understand that the parable is a subsequent comment added by the writer? Where the uncertainty is strong, it has been indicated in the heading (e.g., see no. 50: "perhaps R. Eliezer b. Hyrcanus"; see also nos. 56, 81–82, A1, and A10). In other cases, where no uncertainty is expressed in the parable heading, there is still room for a difference of opinion. In no. 109 the author/editor of Genesis Rabbah reveals his own uncertainty by reporting two conflicting traditions: "R. Judan in the name of R. Johanan b. Zakkai, or R. Berekiah in the name of R. Akiba, said: A parable. It is like a villager. . . ."

Even when a parable is unequivocally attributed to a specific teacher, the question of the accuracy of the attribution remains. This issue is part of the larger question of the accuracy of attribution in rabbinic literature generally. Most of the material passed through a period of oral tradition before acquiring written form. It is well known that the Rabbis developed a methodology for transmitting oral traditions and that they were deeply concerned with the question of original authorship, since the authority of the speaker played a major role in establishing the validity of a teaching. Frequently not only the author of a tradition is identified but also the names of the ones through whom the tradition has been passed down (e.g., in B. Sanhedrin 29a: "R. Abba said in R. Jeremiah's name in Rab's name. . ."). This desire to achieve accuracy in the transmission of a tradition may have been more intense in connection with the halakic, or legal, materials than with haggadic, or nonlegal and homiletic, materials such as the parables. But the great nineteenth-century authority on rabbinic literature, Wilhelm Bacher, affirmed that we cannot doubt the general accuracy of the attributions even in haggadic materials (*Die Agada der Tannaiten*, 2d ed., vol. 1 [1903], p. vi). Even if this positive evaluation is accepted, it is of little help in determining the accuracy of the attribution in the case of any individual parable, which may prove to be an exception to the rule.

The issue is too complex to be explored from all angles here, but there is one piece of evidence from the collection of parables that raises doubts about the accuracy of attribution in this area. Since the same parable is often repeated in more than one source, it is possible to test the consistency in attribution when specific authors are named. Even if three or four sources agree in attributing a given parable to a certain Rabbi, there still remains the possibility that all are wrong, having followed an early but erroneous tradition. On the other hand, when two or more sources disagree as to the author, there is clear evidence of the fallibility of the tradition. They cannot both be right—although, unfortunately, both may be wrong! (One could also argue that both putative authors transmitted a tradition that was older than either, and in that sense both attributions are partially correct, since both were indeed transmitters of the parable.)

Furthermore one cannot assume that a report in an earlier document is necessarily more accurate than one in a later document. Late documents may contain early traditions. There are twenty-five or thirty instances in our collection in which it is possible to test the consistency in attribution of parables (i.e., two or more sources reporting the same parable and providing a specific attribution). In just over half of the cases the attribution in one document is supported by the other documents. To put it negatively: in nearly half of the instances there is an apparent difference of opinion with respect to the authorship of a given parable. The figures given here are not precise, since it is recognized that in some instances there is room for doubt as to the intended attribution. But when allowance has been made for this subjectivity in judgment, it is still clear that in only about half of the cases is the attribution of a parable to a specific author corroborated by the parallel versions of that parable.

Some of the inconsistencies in attribution are intriguing. Thus no. 111 from Genesis Rabbah reports that the parable of the Pearl Lost and Found was told by R. Berekiah b. R. Simon in the name of R. Nehemiah. But the parallel in Ruth R. 8:1 attributes the parable to R. Berekiah and R. Simon. If R. Berekiah b. R. Simon handed on a tradition from R. Nehemiah, it is not surprising that some document ascribes the tradition to him rather than to his predecessor, whom he had been quoting. But how did "R. Berekiah b. R. Simon" become "R. Berekiah and R. Simon"? Or was the patronymic in "R. Berekiah b. R. Simon" incorrect, leading to an attempted improvement? Clearly there has been redactional confusion of some sort.

Another illustration occurs outside the present collection. Pesikta de Rab Kahana 4:4 reports the following "custom of the world" parable:

> R. Levi said in the name of R. Simon b. Menasiah: The very round of Adam's heel outshone the globe of the sun.
>
> And do not wonder at this!
>
> In the custom of the world if a man makes unto himself two salvers, one for himself and one for his steward, whose salver does he make more beautiful? Is it not his own?
>
> Even so Adam was created for the service of the Holy One, blessed be He, and the globe of the sun was created for the service of creatures. It was therefore right that the very round of Adam's heel outshone the globe of the sun. And if the round of Adam's heel outshone the globe of the sun, how much more brightly shone the countenance of his face!

In Eccl. R. 8:1:2, however, the parable is repeated and attributed directly to R. Levi without any reference to his having spoken it in the name of R. Simon b. Menasiah. If R. Levi told the parable, but in the name of R. Simon b. Menasiah, is it right or wrong to attribute it to R. Levi? A number of apparent inconsistencies may be explained by the shift from the originator of a parable to the one who simply repeated it. But even this understanding cannot explain all of the inconsistencies in the attributions. Clearly the names attached to given parables must be used only with caution.

In the headings of the parables in part 1 we have been content to supply the name of the Rabbi to which our source seems to attribute it. We leave it to others to investigate the accuracy of that attribution.

WHEN DID THE PARABLE EMERGE?

The Hebrew noun *mashal,* the rabbinic word for parable, comes from a verb that seems originally to have meant "to liken," a meaning that survives in the passive form "to be/become like" in a number of biblical passages (e.g., Isa. 14:10; Ps. 28:1). In the Old Testament the noun usually means a proverb (as in Ezek. 12:22–23 and throughout the book of Proverbs), but in some cases something very much like an allegory or riddle (e.g., Ezek. 17:2). One gets the impression that the word *mashal* (verb or noun) can refer to almost any artful kind of expression that requires some cleverness or wisdom to utter or to understand. But never in the Old Testament do we find the word applied to the sort of narrative parable the Rabbis later denominated *mashal*; in fact, such parables are not to be found there, though there are a few stories that somewhat resemble them (2 Sam. 12:1–14; 14:5–13; 1 Kings 20:39–42; Isa. 5:1–7; Jer. 13:12–14; and even more remotely Jotham's fable in Judg. 9:7–15).

If the classic rabbinic *mashal* is not anticipated in the Old Testament, when and where did it arise? Although there is some uncertainty, we are safest in concluding that the narrative *mashal*-parable is a creation of Palestine in the first century C.E.

Frequent mention of the *mashal* is made in the Apocryphal book of Ecclesiasticus (1:24; 3:29; 13:26; 20:20, 27; 21:16; 38:33; 39:2, 3; 47:15 [LXX]/17 [Heb.]) and in the pseudepigraphical book of 1 Enoch. In the former it perhaps means proverb, though it is often coupled with the word for riddle (as is true also in Ezek. 17:2); in the latter (where Aramaic fragments of the work use the Aramaic equivalent *matlah*), the meaning is oration, discourse, or vision. Neither do we find the rabbinic *mashal* in the literature from Qumran.

The Greco-Roman parable also differs from the rabbinic *mashal*, though it may have had some influence upon it. In fact, David Flusser (*Die rabbinische Gleichnisse und der Gleichniserzähler Jesus*, pt. 1 [Bern: Peter Lang, 1981], pp. 141–60) argues that the Hellenistic fables and illustrations used by popular philosophers may have been the germ from which the Palestinian *mashal* evolved. Here one thinks of the Socratic parables of The Hunter Who Frightens the Game (Plato, *Lysis* 2) and The Intelligent Gardener (*Phaedrus* 61). Xenophon attributed to Prodicus The Parable of Virtue and Vice, represented by an attractive and a loathsome woman meeting Hercules at a crossroads (*Memorabilia* 2.1.21–34), which was cited again by Justin Martyr in the name of Xenophon (2 *Apology* 11).

Aristotle discussed example, parable, and fable in his *Rhetoric* 2.20. He understood the parable to be "a comparison and application of cases easily supposable and such as occur in real life, for the purpose of illustrating the point in question; the fable, on the other hand, is pure fiction" (*The "Art" of Rhetoric, by Aristotle*, Loeb Classical Library, trans. John Henry Freese [Cambridge, Mass.: Harvard University

Press, 1947], p. 274n). Aristotle thus explains: "Parable is illustrated by the sayings of Socrates; for instance, if one were to say that magistrates should not be chosen by lot, for this would be the same as choosing as representative athletes not those competent to contend, but those on whom the lot falls; or as choosing any of the sailors as the man who should take the helm, as if it were right that the choice should be decided by lot, not by a man's knowledge."

An example of a Roman parable, The Parable of the Stomach, is found in Livy, *History of Rome* 2.32. As we read all these examples, we notice that they are sometimes more complicated and allegorical, but they are totally lacking in the sort of stereotyped formulary or structure that marks the rabbinic parables. Parables as well as fables of Indian provenience were known in the Greco-Roman world and also to the Rabbis. But unless Flusser's conjecture finds better support, none of these sources helps us very much in our quest.

In the Apocryphal book of 4 Ezra (or 2 Esdras), there is an example of a parable that closely resembles the rabbinic kind (8:1–3).

> The Most High made this world for the sake of many,
> but the world to come for the sake of few.
>
> But I will tell you a parable [*Dicam autem coram te similitudinem*], Ezra. Just as, when you ask the earth, it will tell you that it provides very much clay from which earthenware is made, but only a little dust from which gold comes; so is the course of the present world.

This source survives only in a Latin translation of a Greek translation of the original Hebrew or Aramaic. The formula that introduces the parable surely represents (at second remove) the early rabbinic introductory formula *emshol lak mashal* (cf., e.g., nos. 17–18). The book of 4 Ezra was composed in Palestine toward the end of the first century C.E. (See also 4 Ezra 4:21–42, 50; 5:42, 48; 7:10, 60, 105, etc.)

By that date the narrative *mashal* was already a popular teaching device among the Rabbis of Palestine. Who or what was responsible for this efflorescence of narrative parabolic teaching? Some have seen the teaching method of Jesus as the stimulus, and it is true that his parables are the earliest narrative *meshalim* attested in literature. Joachim Jeremias even goes as far as to say that "Jesus' parables are . . .

something completely new" (*Die Gleichnisse Jesu*, 8th ed. [Göttingen: Vandenhoeck and Ruprecht, 1970], p. 8). Others stress Hellenistic influence, especially the first-century dissemination of the Aesopic and Indian fables. While these may have been an influence, they are clearly something different from the typical rabbinic *mashal*. The nonattestation of any close formal parallels elsewhere lends weight to the assumption that the Palestinian *mashal* was probably homegrown.

Still others claim that our genre can be traced to Hillel and Shammai, teachers in the early first century, or to the first generation of Tannaim, all of whom were contemporary with Jesus. But few if any parables come down to us from Hillel, Shammai, or the first generation of Tannaim, and such items as we have are not true *meshalim*, and their authenticity is contested (see, e.g., no. A8). We must remember, however, that the calamity that descended upon Palestinian Judaism in 70 C.E. resulted in the loss of much oral and written tradition.

Another possible explanation is that Jesus and the Rabbis both simply took up and used a popular form they found on the lips of common people in the streets. But there is no way to confirm this history, and it does not tell us how the popular form originated.

If we limit ourselves to what we can know from the records (and if we accept them at face value), we can say only this much: The first known teacher who used narrative parables of the *mashal* type was Jesus. The Israeli scholar Pinchas Lapide suggests an interesting theory to explain the statement in Matthew 7:29, "He taught them as one who had authority, and not as their scribes." Lapide assumes that Matthew's Greek is based on a Hebrew source that may have read, "He taught them as a parablist. . . ." The Hebrew word *ke-moshel* could be taken as either "as a ruler" or "as a parabler." (See Lapide, "A Panel of Commentary on Petuchowski's Discussion of the Parable," *Christian News from Israel*, n.s., 23 [1972–73]: 148.)

From R. Johanan b. Zakkai (ca. 70 C.E.) onward, if attributions are to be trusted, parables become increasingly more common. Certain Rabbis, such as Johanan and Meir, seem to have been especially noted for their use of them. (See Introduction).

As noted in the Introduction, *mashal*-parabling remained

an almost exclusively Palestinian practice. It did not take root
elsewhere. The Babylonian Rabbis seem scarcely to have
made parables. The ancient Christian scholar Jerome, who
learned Hebrew from a Rabbi and resided thirty-four years in
Palestine in the late fourth and early fifth centuries, re-
marked: "It is common among the Syrians, and especially
the Palestinians, to connect parables to all their discourses,
so that that which might not be grasped by the listeners
might through simple precept be grasped, through similitudes and examples" (*Commentariorum in Evangelium Matthaei*
18:23 [Migne Petrologia Latina, 26.137b]).

But while others elsewhere seem to have been unable to
produce *meshalim* of their own, they were happy enough to
import the products of Palestine, so that parables are
scattered throughout the Babylonian Talmud, and indeed
throughout all the classical rabbinic literature until the
Middle Ages. One very early parable found its way into the
letter of the late first-century Christian bishop, Clement of
Rome (1 Clement 23:3–4; cf. 2 Clement 11:2–5). But except
when they are citing the parables of Jesus, the early Christian
fathers used the word *parable* for something quite different.
For them it meant a mystical type, a dark saying, an allegory,
a vision—in short, something that needed to be decoded.
They did not know how to compose parables like those of
Jesus and the Rabbis.

So striking is this inability of the genre to be trans-
planted that we can be bold and say that wherever we
encounter an example of it, the overwhelming probability is
that the item came from Palestine originally and must be
dated sometime after the beginning of the first century c.e.,
and fairly probably before the eighth.

2

THE STRUCTURE OF
RABBINIC PARABLES

It may be recalled from chapter 1 that the classical narrative *mashal* in its fullest form consisted of five distinguishable parts. Many specimens lack one or two of these parts, but the typical one has all five. In this chapter we give a condensed overview of these parts. More detailed examination of them will occupy subsequent chapters.

THE ILLUSTRAND

The illustrand is simply the matter to be illustrated, proved, or explained. Strictly speaking, it is not directly a part of the parable structurally, but it is the immediate context of the parable and its reason for existence. It is therefore a part of the parabolic pericope in the broader sense. It is a rare parable that has no explicit illustrand.

While parables are by their nature haggadic (homiletic, or dealing with theological opinion), they theoretically could be enlisted in the service of halakah (legal points). But the vast majority of them illustrate matters that could only be described as haggadah. Nevertheless, a number of our items are employed to establish halakic principles, such as no. 80. Rabbi Ishmael b. Elisha, in a discussion of the trial by ordeal in Numbers 5:11–31, reports a sort of parable that is itself part of a legal procedure and could therefore almost be called a halakic parable (Sifre on Numbers 12).

> R. Ishmael says: First he tells her about the power of the bitter water. He says to her:
>
> My daughter, I say to you: This bitter water, unto what is it like? It is like some dry poisonous medicine, which if placed on ordinary flesh does no damage; but when it is placed on an open wound, it begins to eat away at it.
>
> Even so, you, if you are pure, drink and do not refuse; for "you shall be free from this water of bitterness" (Num. 5:19).

Illustrands can also be classified in general terms of the types of subject matter illustrated, proved, or explained. By far the largest number of preserved specimens are exegetical; that is, the illustrands are texts of scriptural interpretations, as in no. 38. David Flusser believes that this use of parables arose after 120 C.E., in the time of Rabbi Akiba, while earlier they illustrated ethical demands, their theme being the religious meaning of human life, the conduct of man before God (*Rabbinische Gleichnisse und Gleichniserzähler Jesus* [Bern: Peter Lang, 1981], pt. 1, pp. 21–39). No. 19 is thus an example of the older type of illustrand, as are the parables of Jesus. But the surviving evidence is too sparse to allow certainty on this hypothesis. In fact, if attributions are to be trusted, among the oldest parables coming down to us— ascribed to the Schools of Hillel and Shammai—are nos. 108–9, which are purely exegetical parables.

But many illustrands may be called historical, dealing with events rather than texts as such. To be sure, most of the events are biblical, as nos. 37 and 39 illustrate. Other illustrands could be called moral, dealing with a duty (e.g., no. 78). Obviously, some duties are pegged to texts, so that items such as no. 63 could be classified in more than one way. A fairly large number of items may be classified as theological or philosophical (e.g., no. 49). A dozen or so illustrands may be described as prudential (e.g., no. 95). Others can be called legal, if that category can be distinguished from moral.

THE INTRODUCTORY FORMULA

The story part of the parable is typically prefixed by words such as "They parable a parable. Unto what is the matter like? It is like unto. . . ." This formula is a long one; frequently only the last part or last two parts of this formula is used. (See chapter 3.)

It is necessary to report here a serious problem in translating the Hebrew. Some of the most common introductory formulas are difficult to construe, and their proper vocalization and translation has been subject to debate. This is particularly the case with the phrase that we have translated, "they parable a parable." This expression is clearly a verbal form followed by a cognate accusative, which can be seen also in the Old Testament (Ezek. 12:23; 17:2; 24:3). The problem is how to construe and translate the verbal form. The two best options are either to vocalize the Hebrew as *mashlu mashal* and translate "they parabled a parable" or "they parable a parable," or (as Wilhelm Bacher advocated) to vocalize as *moshlo mashal* and translate as an imperative, "tell him a parable!" Either rendering sounds dissonant to the modern reader, since there is no antecedent for either the "they" or the "him." But since we find Bacher's arguments for the second option unconvincing upon closer examination, we have chosen to follow the first option, which may be an example of the so-called impersonal use of the third-person plural, a typically Semitic periphrastic passive that might be freely translated, "a parable is told."

THE PARABLE PROPER

The story thus introduced constitutes the "illustration half" (Jülicher's *Bildhälfte*) of the parabolic unit. The narrative may be either about a specific event expressible in English with verbs in the past tense (e.g., no. 12) or about an everyday occurrence or general situation describable with verbs in the present tense (e.g., nos. 7 and 10). The Hebrew does not always permit us to distinguish sharply between these two kinds of illustrations.

The word or word group that appears in the formula "It is like unto an X that . . ." may be called a comparison word. Although one might logically expect that the person or thing thus introduced at the beginning of the story would continue to occupy the center of attention as the principal object to which the actuality is compared, such is not always the case. For example, no. 85 begins, "It is like a king who gave to his servant a field. . . ." The rest of the story, however, is not about the king but about the servant. This phenomenon, which Paul Fiebig called "a shifting of the center of gravity," and which G. V. Jones called "a transference of the point of comparison," will be further discussed in chapter 3.

THE APPLICATION

The great majority of rabbinic parables attach to the story an explicit interpretation or application of it, making the point quite clear. This part of the parabolic unit is usually introduced by the word *kak* (even so; likewise).

CITATION OF SCRIPTURE

To the application is frequently appended one or several scriptural quotations intended to clinch the point, usually introduced by a formula such as "as it is said. . . ." In our presentation of parables in part 1, we have put in separate paragraphs the three main sections of the parabolic unit: (1) the illustrand; (2) the parable proper, prefixed by its introductory formula; and (3) the application, introduced by a linking word (usually *kak*) and sometimes supported by scriptural citation.

FUNCTION

We have analyzed the typical rabbinic *mashal*-parable into its five parts. It may now be appropriate to append some remarks about the function of the parabolic unit as a whole. Viewed in relation to their present literary contexts, the great majority of the rabbinic parables that have been preserved for us can be called exegetical—they are most often employed to explain a text, incident, or narrative in the Scriptures. Viewed in relation to their original audiences, as far as these can be determined, the parables may be polemic or didactic, though these categories may overlap.

Another way of approaching the function of our parables is to note their purpose in relation to their illustrands. Very commonly, rabbinic parables may illustrate, clarify, or elucidate a text, as in no. 38. Sometimes the illustrand is a biblical event (no. 37), or perhaps (but rarely) a natural phenomenon or biographic event. This function is sometimes accomplished by amplification (no. 46), exemplification (no. 56), or elaboration (no. 88).

Frequently a parable serves as a species of proof in a polemic context (nos. 60–61), often used analogously with a proof text. This use is closely related to another—the resolution of a perplexity, as in nos. 57 and 89. The perplexity may be in the area of a seeming contradiction in Scripture; theodicy; reflections against a biblical hero, against Israel, or against conventional values; or some similar threat to the intellectual understanding or moral sensibility. In such cases the illustrand poses a problem or asks a question, and the parable seeks to resolve it (no. 50). The analogy of such a use of parables to proof texts can be seen in an argument of Rabbi Joshua the grits dealer (Soferim 1:2):

> One question asked to R. Joshua the grits dealer: Why is it permitted to write (sacred scrolls) on the skins of *nebeloth* [animals that died of natural causes] and *terefoth* [animals that died of disease]?
>
> He said to him: I will parable to thee a parable. Unto what is the matter like? It is like unto the case of two men who were condemned to death by the state, one being executed by the king, and the other by the executioner. Which of them is superior? He who was executed by the king.
>
> The other said to him: If so, they should be permitted to be eaten. R. Joshua said to him: It says: "Ye shall not eat any *nebelah*" (Deut. 14:21). Scripture has forbidden it, so what can I do for you?

In a very general way, it may be observed that virtually all rabbinic parables serve to reinforce conventional values. Perhaps the only possible exception to this rule in the items studied is nos. 22–23, which seem to involve an attack on the idea of human merits. This observation is significant because a recent school of thought in parable study has defined the genre in terms of its reversing conventional values or making "a raid on the rational." Such a definition of parables arises from concentrating exclusively on certain parables of Jesus, but its inapplicability to rabbinic parables can be underscored by contrasting the rabbinic parable of the Exceptional

Laborer (no. 68) with Matthew 20:1–16, the Parable of the Generous Employer.

If a really striking difference between the parables of the Rabbis and those of Jesus is to be sought, it must be sought in this contrast between the purposes for which they were used: while the rabbinic parables seek to reinforce conventional values, those of Jesus tend to undermine or invert them. The parables of the Rabbis seek to resolve perplexities, but those of Jesus create them. The parables of the Rabbis intend to make life and thought smoother, but those of Jesus make them harder. It is the upsetting quality of the typical gospel parable that provides the clearest contrast with that of the rabbinic literature. Jesus the parabler was a subversive.

3

INTRODUCTORY
FORMULAS

In his study of early rabbinic parables Theodor Gutt-mann listed seventy-five different introductory formulas but then reduced that number to twenty-three significant items (*Das Mashal-Gleichnis in tannaitischer Zeit* [Frankfurt am Main: Hermon, 1929], pp. 3–6). The situation may be further simplified by noting that in this collection, and in rabbinic parables generally, the dominant introductory formula is tripartite, with slight variations. The first section of the formula identifies the literary genre that is to follow. In its briefest form it says simply, "A parable" (e.g., nos. 40–42). Expanded variations are "I will parable you a parable" (nos. 16–18) or "They parable a parable" (nos. 33, 35–36).

The second section of the tripartite formula consists of a rhetorical question, normally, "Unto what is the matter like?" (nos. 38–40). Occasionally this rhetorical question is modified so as to clarify the point under discussion, for example, "Unto what is the evil inclination like?" (no. 32), or "Unto what was Israel like at that moment?" (no. 43), or "Unto whom is Moses our teacher like?" (Ruth R. Introductory section 5). These variants, however, are a very small proportion of the total occurrences.

The third section of the tripartite formula responds to the rhetorical question and is attached to the opening word in the story half of the parable: "It is like a man . . ." (no. 17) or, frequently, "It is like a king . . . " (nos. 5, 14, 16). A review of the parables indicates that the first item in the story half is not necessarily the central issue in the comparison. A cumbersome but accurate way to paraphrase the third section of the introduction would be, "It is like the situation in which a king. . . ." Thus in parable no. 55 the point of the story is found in the king's triumph over robbers and the reestablishment of his authority, but the story half begins, "It is like robbers . . ." rather than, "It is like a king who. . . ."

The full tripartite introductory formula occurs in about half of the parables in this collection. The proportion would be substantially higher except for the curious fact that Sifre on Deuteronomy, with only a few exceptions, uses the first and third elements of the full formula while omitting the second (e.g., see nos. 85–87). A third of our 115 parables follow the shortened introductory formula preferred by Sifre on Deuteronomy. It is worth noting that where only the first and third elements of the full formula are used, the first element is regularly the simple form "A parable" rather than the more complex "I will parable you a parable" or "They parable a parable." No. 37 is the one exception to this rule and raises the possibility that the present text is not correct. If one examines the entire 325 parables of Johnston's dissertation, the percentages are slightly lower for the full tripartite introduction and for the use of the first and third elements without the rhetorical question (35 percent and 26 percent respectively). But these two forms far exceed the other variants.

It would be useful to be able to trace the development of the tripartite formula. For example, was the earliest introduction the simple "It is like . . ."? And were the other elements added later? If so, which section was added first, and which later? The difficulty in answering these questions arises in part from the difficulty of dating the rabbinic documents. But a larger part derives from our awareness that practically all of these materials passed through a period of oral development and subsequently a period of development at the written stage. In details of the introduction the final form may reflect the taste of the final editor or of some transmitter of the tradition along the way. Reference has already been made to the comparative paucity of tripartite introductions in Sifre on Deuteronomy. Again, in Genesis Rabbah there are no occurrences of the tripartite introduction in our sample of six parables or in the sixteen that appear in Johnston's larger work.

Furthermore, when the same parable appears in two or three documents, there are sometimes differences in the introductory formulas used. Thus no. 40 (The Slave and the Rotten Fish) has a tripartite introduction in Mekilta, but the version in Pesikta de Rab Kahana 11:3 begins immediately, "It is like a king who said to his slave. . . ." Similarly no. 41 (The Cheaply Sold Field) in Mekilta begins with the tripartite introduction, but the same parable in Pesikta de Rab Kahana 11:7 begins, "It is like one to whom there fell an inheritance. . . ." A review of the documents involved reveals that the Mekilta has a strong preference for the tripartite introduction, while the Pesikta of Rab Kahana favors the simpler introduction. There are numerous other examples of this phenomenon, though there are also instances in which three or four versions of the same parable are introduced in the same fashion. See no. 39 (The Escape from Three Perils), which is from Mekilta; there are parallels in Tosefta Berakoth 1:11, B. Berakoth 13a, and P. Berakoth 1:9. All four versions use the tripartite introduction.

The Mishnah is the earliest rabbinic document extant. It reached substantially its present form through the work of R. Judah ha-Nasi at the beginning of the third century C.E. But some changes or additions were made even after that time; M. Sotah 9:15, for example, refers to the death of R. Judah ha-Nasi ("When Rabbi died, humility and the shunning of sin ceased"). Since this earliest rabbinic document was a codification of Jewish law, it made very little use of parables (but see nos. 1–4 and A7). The full tripartite formula is used in no. 1, while nos. 2–4 follow a somewhat different pattern, but one that includes essentially the second and third items of the full formula. It is probably safe to assume that the tripartite formula was in use by the beginning of the third century C.E. This dating is confirmed by the prevalence of this form in the Mekilta and Tosefta, since these documents contain predominantly Tannaitic material, although they were not completed until around 400 C.E.

But is there any evidence that the introductory formulas existed or were developing during the first and second centuries C.E., that is, prior to the end of the Tannaitic period? The earliest parables relevant for the present purpose are those attributed to the competing schools of Hillel and Shammai and those assigned to R. Johanan b. Zakkai. The latter was active before and after the Jewish-Roman War of 66–73 C.E., while the schools flourished at least until this war and possibly even later. The parables from the schools were used in support of their differing views as to whether the heavens or the earth was created first. As reported in Genesis R. 1:15 (nos. 107–8), each began its parable, "A parable. It is like a king who. . . ." The same two-part introduction appears also in the same parables as reported in the parallel passage in Leviticus R. 31:1. The parables are repeated also in P. Hagigah 2:1 and the introductions.

Of the four parables in this collection attributed to Johanan b. Zakkai, two (nos. 13–14) begin with a tripartite introduction, while the other two (nos. 19 and 109) begin, "A parable. It is like. . . ." Variations in the introductions of the parallels are a reminder that the extant texts do not necessarily reflect the language of the original creators of the parables.

The prevalence of a tripartite introduction in the rabbinic parables is distinctive. This usage was almost certainly in existence by the end of the Tannaitic period, but it is not possible to determine how much earlier it may have emerged.

4

THE STORIES
THEY TOLD

THE KING PARABLES

The stories that appear in the rabbinic parables reflect a wide variety of interests, but even the casual reader notes the predominance of the king figures. In Ignaz Ziegler's *Die Königsgleichnisse des Midrasch beleuchtet durch die römische Kaiserzeit* (Breslau: Schlesische Verlags-Anstalt v. S. Schoetlaender, 1903), nearly a thousand parables or parable-like illustrations are cited using the figure of a king. More than half of Johnston's 325 parables fall in this category, and a survey of the entire file of 1,500 items supports the view that half of all rabbinic parables involve the figure of the king. Sometimes this is the case even when nothing in the story or its interpretation hinges on that particular role. For example, it is not evident that no. 64 is strengthened or made more relevant by the fact that the woman involved is "a king's daughter." It is likely that the prominence of the king figure was due partly to the assumed appropriateness of the king as a symbol for God, partly to the glamor that the king and his court added to any story, and perhaps partly to the fact that once the king motif had been established as a convention, it was often followed without any deliberate decision.

An interesting aspect of the king parables is that in a

number of instances one version of a parable involves a king, while in another version the king figure does not appear. The chart below illustrates this difference between the various versions of a number of parables. Parables from the present collection are cited by number, and the name of the document is included also to assist in making comparisons. In the first seven examples, the version appearing in part 1 includes the king; in the next four, our version does not have the king. The final example does not appear in part 1.

Parable	With King	Without King
6. The Lamp Removed	Tos. Sukkah	B. Sukkah
34. The Palace with a Tannery Pipe	ARNa; Kallah Rabbati	Derek Eretz R.
60. The Dog Named After Father	B. Abodah Zarah	Mek. Bachodesh
86. The Great Inheritance	Sifre on Deut.	Sifre on Deut.
87. The Woman Who Ate Forbidden Figs	Sifre on Deut.	Sifre on Num.; B. Yoma; Numbers R.
93. The Medicinal Plaster	Sifre on Deut.	B. Kiddushin
94. The Precious Bird	Sifre on Deut.; ARNa; ARNb	B. Menahoth
25. The Aborted Wedding Celebration	Genesis R.	B. Sanhedrin
27. The Curious Wife and the Scorpion	ARNb; Pirqe de R. Eliezer	ARNa; Genesis R.
40. The Slave and the Rotten Fish	Pesikta de Rab Kahana	Mek. Beshallach
44. The Superfluous Mediator	Exodus R.	Mek. Beshallach
– Three Sureties Required	Song R. 1:4:1	Midrash on Ps. 8:4

A review of the versions with and without the king figure does not provide any clear evidence as to whether earlier or later writers preferred the use of this symbol. The frequency of the king figure is relatively high, however, in

Sifra on Leviticus and in Sifre on Numbers and Deuteronomy (over 70 percent in each), and relatively low in Mekilta (under 50 percent), and lower still in Tosefta (35 percent). The two versions of Aboth de Rabbi Nathan probably have the lowest percentages of all. (The figure of the king does not occur in any of the parables or parable-like sayings in the Mishnah, but the parabolic material is so limited in this document that the evidence is of limited significance.) With the aid of a computer it might be possible to draw some conclusions after examining all versions of all the parables in all the relevant literature, but as yet no definite pattern has emerged. At best, it could be argued that the incidence of king parables is slightly higher in the later rabbinic documents. There is one interesting case in which the lead figure is identified simply as "a man who had a field." Later in the story, however, there appears unexpectedly the rhetorical question, "With whom is the king angry?" indicating that the owner has been elevated to royalty (Exod. R. 27:9). The reader suspects that the writer began simply with "a man" and then unconsciously shifted to the conventional king figure. Since the interpretation relates the lead figure to God, it was easy for the writer to turn the owner of the field into a king.

In the great majority of cases the king in the parable story does indeed represent God. There are, however, a few surprising exceptions. In the Parable of the Curious Wife and the Scorpion (no. 27), the husband is identified as a man. (See also Gen. R. 19:10). But in the Pirqe de R. Eliezer 13 and in version B of Aboth de R. Nathan 1, he is presented as a king. The curious feature of these four versions is that where the husband is called a man, it is the wife who parallels Adam in the interpretation; but in the version in which the husband is identified as a king, it is explicitly stated that the king represents Adam and the wife is Eve. Again, in no. 48 the interpretation equates the king with the ministering angels that attacked the Egyptians once the Israelites were safely across the sea. (This identification may not be so surprising, since, we could say, the ministering angels and God are on the same side of the divide between heavenly and earthly beings. In no. 80 the king corresponds with the high priest of the interpretation. In no. 98 the king apparently represents Moses and not God. Perhaps most surprising is no. 102, in which the king is rescued by "a certain brave man"; here the king is Abraham, and the brave man is God. (Admittedly it would have been even more surprising if Abraham had been described as rescuing God!) In Sifre on Deuteronomy 352 the king apparently represents Jacob, and the favorite son is Benjamin. These instances are significant exceptions to the general pattern.

Since the king is the most common figure in the parables, it is natural that members of his family and the royal entourage should also appear frequently. In the largest number of instances, it is his son or sons who appear with him. Next in order of frequency are his wife or betrothed, or a woman considered for that role. Almost as numerous are parables that involve his daughter or daughters. In addition there are parables in which the king appears along with various officials of his court or army, and then (slightly less frequently) parables in which the king is involved with his subjects or territories. In parallel fashion there are parables in which the lead figure is a man as father or husband, and again he is frequently involved with his son(s), daughter(s), wife, servants, workers, and so on.

ANIMAL PARABLES OR FABLES

Parables that do not involve either kings or fathers are difficult to group together, since they are so diverse, but one or two classifications stand out clearly enough to attract attention. While not numerous, there are a number of animal parables or fables. The most distinctive is the Parable of the Fox and the Fishes (no. 18). It is widely held that this story was adopted by R. Akiba from Hellenistic or even Indian sources. While fables in rabbinic literature do not normally use the parable format, either R. Akiba or a later editor has provided this fable with the tripartite introductory formula and the attached interpretation. Two other fables appear in the appendix: The Fox That Offered to Appease the Lion (no. A5), and The Fox That Fasted, Feasted, and Fasted (no. A6).

Another such fable is attributed to R. Joshua b. Hananiah. On some occasion the Jewish community threatened revolt against the Roman government because of an especially objectionable regulation. The leaders wished to avoid such a revolt and sent the Rabbi to address the people. He told the following story:

A wild lion killed (an animal), and a bone stuck in his throat. Thereupon he proclaimed, "I will reward anyone who removes it." An Egyptian heron, which has a long beak, came and pulled it out and demanded his reward. "Go," he replied, "you will be able to boast that you entered the lion's mouth in peace and came out in peace." Even so, let us be satisfied that we entered into dealings with this people in peace and have emerged in peace. (Gen. R. 64:10)

Still another such fable-parable, this one provided with a regular *mashal*-type introduction, occurs in B. Sanhedrin 98b–99a:

R. Simlai expounded: What is meant by "Woe unto you that desire the day of the Lord! To what end is it for you? The day of the Lord is darkness and not light" [Amos 5:18].

A parable. This is like a cock and a bat who were hopefully waiting for the light [of dawn]. The cock said to the bat: I look forward to the light because I have sight; but of what use is the light to you?

And thus a *min* [heretic] said to R. Abbahu: When will the messiah come? He replied: When darkness covers those people. You curse me, he exclaimed. He retorted: It is but a verse: "For behold the darkness shall cover the earth, and gross darkness the people; but the Lord shall shine upon thee, and His glory shall be upon thee" (Isa. 60:2).

See also The Dog in the Baker's Shop (Gen. R. 22:6); The Head and the Tail of the Serpent (Deut. R. 1:10); The Caged Bird (Eccl. R. 11:9:1); The Sow, the She-ass, and the Filly (Est. R. 7:1); The Lion's Banquet and the Fox (7:3).

Still other parables use animals as central characters, but the stories are not so clearly in the style of the fable, since the animals do not talk (except perhaps to themselves). See nos. 43 and 84. A saying that is more proverb than parable is reported in Mek. Bachodesh 7:63–65. It was intended to teach that the Sabbath should be both anticipated and remembered. The comment was made in connection with Exodus 20:9, which commands observance of the Sabbath:

Remember it before it comes, and observe it after it has gone. . . . Hence they said: We should always increase what is holy by adding to it some of the nonholy. . . . A parable. It is like a wolf who moves backward and forward.

In Exodus R. 5:12 there is an equally brief animal metaphor attributed to R. Akiba.

> Why is Israel compared to a bird? Just as a bird can fly only with its wings, so Israel can survive only with the help of its elders.

For other parables or parable-like sayings involving animals, see Ruth Proem 5; Leviticus R. 13:2; P. Hagigah 1:1; Midrash on Psalms 90:3.

WISDOM PARABLES

Another group of parables may be tentatively classed together as wisdom parables because they agree in describing true scholars and their opposites. Not many have been included in this collection because they differ slightly in their format from the standard parable form, as we have defined it (but see nos. 2–4, 20, A9). The majority of these parables are twin or geminate parables and deal with two contrasting types of persons. They tend not to use people for their symbols but inanimate objects such as trees, grapes, wine, paper and ink, stones, and so forth, though there are exceptions, such as ARNa 23:4:

> Rabban Simeon b. Gamaliel. . . . He who learns Torah in his youth is like a young man who married a virgin: they suit one another and desire one another. But he who learns Torah in his old age is like an old man who married a virgin: she suits him, but he does not suit her; she desires him, but he withdraws from her. [See also the parable that follows in the same section.]

It is striking that the great majority of parables of this type appear in the Mishnah tractate Aboth and in the Aboth de Rabbi Nathan (see chaps. 4, 18, 23–24, 26–28, 40–41). Such parables are less numerous in Recension B of Aboth de Rabbi Nathan, but see chapters 18, 34–35. These geminate, wisdom parables are less frequent in the other rabbinic literature, but they do occur, as in no. 24 (B. Kiddushin). See also Exodus R. 36:3 on the man who finds the light of Torah and the man who does not, Midrash on Psalms 27:2 on the wicked and the righteous, and 119:44 on the same basic theme. In the Pirqe de R. Eliezer 25 there is an attractive parable commenting on the phrase "He who walks with the wise men shall be wise; but the companion of fools shall be broken" (Prov. 13:20).

"He who walks with wise men shall be wise."

To what is this like? To one who enters a perfumer's shop, although he neither takes anything nor gives anything, nevertheless he absorbs a good scent, and goes away (therewith).

Likewise everyone who walks with the righteous acquires some of their good ways and deeds . . . , "but the companion of fools shall be broken."

Unto what is this like? To a man who enters a tannery, although he neither takes nor gives anything, nevertheless he has absorbed a foul odor. Likewise he who walks with the wicked acquires something of their evil ways and deeds.

THE USE OF RHETORICAL QUESTIONS

Perhaps the most interesting minor stylistic device in the story half of the rabbinic parables is the occasional use there of a rhetorical question. Such questions are raised not by one of the characters in the story but by the storyteller himself, who interrupts the narrative to address the audience, a kind of aside that focuses the listeners' curiosity while delaying its satisfaction. In no. 26 there are two such interruptions of the narrative: "What did that man do?" and "What did that proselyte say in her heart?" Again in no. 27 there are two similar rhetorical questions: "What did the man do?" and "What did the woman do?" In no. 89 occurs the question, "Why did he say that?" and in no. 90 the brief "How then?" In no. 49 there again occurs "What did he do?" See also the questions in nos. 60–61 and A6.

Perhaps the most extreme example of this device occurs in Pesikta Rabbati 49:7, where the ten plagues on the Egyptians are compared with the military tactics of a king.

The Holy One, blessed be He, moved against the Egyptians with the tactics of a king in command of his army. How so? In the way of the world, when a province rebels against a king, what does the king do to it? He first shuts off its water. So did the Holy One, blessed be He. He first turned the Egyptians' water into blood, as it is said. . . .

What does a king do next? He brings up trumpeters to sound a warning against the province. Even thus the Holy One, blessed be He, brought frogs against Egypt to serve as trumpeters of a warning against Pharaoh, as it is said. . . . What does a king do next to the rebellious province? . . .

It is scarcely necessary to continue the quotation through the entire ten plagues, each section of the narrative being introduced with "What does a king do next?" followed by reference to a military tactic and then the alleged analogy with one of the plagues. Admittedly this parable rather overdoes the device of the rhetorical question, since the development of the narrative becomes monotonously predictable—though perhaps ingenious.

A more typical use of the device is found in Genesis R. 8:10, where the rhetorical question occurs both in the story half and in the interpretation.

R. Hoshaya said: When the Holy One, blessed be He, created Adam, the ministering angels mistook him for a divine being and wished to exclaim "Holy" before him. Unto what is the matter like? It is like a king and a governor who sat in a chariot, and his subjects wished to say to the king, "Domine! (Sovereign)!" but they did not know which one he was. *What did the king do?* He pushed the governor out of the chariot, and so they knew who was the king. Similarly, when the Lord created Adam, the angels mistook him for a divine being. *What did the Holy One, blessed be He, do?* He caused sleep to fall upon him, and so all knew that he was but mortal man.

A review of Johnston's 325 parables indicates that 12 percent of the parables reflect the use of this rhetorical device in some form, though in the larger collection of 1,500 items the percentage is somewhat higher. The difference may not be statistically significant but does suggest that the usage is slightly more common in the later writings. The most frequent form of the question was, What did (does) X do (say)? But the same motif is expressed in other ways. In no. 12, for example, the narrator invites the verdict of the listeners with the question, "Whose punishment will be the greater?" before completing the story.

Lest the significance of this usage in the story half of some rabbinic parables be overestimated, it is appropriate to point out that rhetorical questions—and specifically, "What did X do?"—appear fairly frequently in rabbinic literature both in narrative sections and in argumentation, for example in the commentaries. Thus in Pesikta Rabbati 32:3/4 there occurs the question, "What did R. Johanan do?" or in Ecclesiastes R. 4:8:5 about R. Simeon, "What did he do?"; and in the Pirqe de R. Eliezer 23 there are at least four occurrences: "What did Noah do?" "What did they do?" "What did Noah do?" and "What did the Holy One, blessed be He, do?" Variants on the question appear frequently in the Mekilta as a device to keep the discussion continuing (e.g., "Why was this said?" "Where had he said it?" etc.). See Mek. Piska 12:60–61; 13:1–2, 67; 15:41–42, 48, 60, 99, 131, and others. The rhetorical question was a common device that appears in parables as well as elsewhere.

GEMINATE AND "TWIN" PARABLES

In this category are instances in which two parables, or two halves of one parable, are parallel in structure but depict contrasted persons, situations, or forms of behavior. See nos. 2–4, 9–10, 30, A9. We think it best to reserve the term *twin* for two parallel but distinct parables and to use the term *geminate* to describe one parable with two parallel halves. In one instance the twins have become triplets:

> They asked R. Johanan b. Zakkai: One who is wise and fears sin, what is he? He said to them: Behold, he is a craftsman who has the tools of his craft in his hand.
>
> One who is wise but does not fear sin, what is he? He said to them: Behold, he is a craftsman who has not the tools of his craft in his hand.
>
> One who fears sin but is not wise, what is he? He said to them: Behold, he is no craftsman, but the tools of his craft are in his hand. (Aboth de R. Nathan 22:1)

Twenty-three such twin parables have been noted among the 325 of the Johnston collection, and several others are close to this pattern but lack the full-scale antithetical parallelism (e.g., Gen. R. 30:10, with the parable attributed to R. Nehemiah contrasting Noah and Abraham).

It is noteworthy that in these twin parables the introduction normally does not have the first item of the standard tripartite introduction (i.e., "A parable" or some such statement). The second item of the standard introduction does occur but in the form "To what are the righteous like?" instead of "To what is the matter like?" And since the introduction has already made explicit the point to be explained by the parable, there is generally no interpretation attached, though there may be a Scripture quotation to climax the presentation. The bulk of these twin parables are in two documents: the Aboth of the Mishnah, and the Aboth de Rabbi Nathan. Both of these documents contain predominantly Tannaitic (i.e., early) materials.

When one turns to the later materials, there is an almost complete absence of this type of parable, though a few exceptions approach the twin-parable form, for example, the Midrash on Psalms 1:20:

> Commenting on "I am . . . the lily of the valley" (Song 2:1).
>
> R. Eleazar said: The righteous are likened to the most exquisite plant and to its most exquisite variety: the most exquisite plant, the lily; its most exquisite variety, the lily of the valley: not the lily of the mountain, which soon withers, but the lily of the valley, which blossoms again and again.
>
> But the wicked, they are likened to the vilest thing and to its vilest representative: the vilest thing is chaff, for it is said of the wicked, "Let them be as chaff before the wind" (Ps. 35:5). It is written further, "The wicked are not so, but are like the chaff which the wind driveth away" (1:4). Do not suppose that the wicked are likened to the chaff of the valley that contains some moisture! No, they are like the chaff of the mountains, which the wind driveth away.

Other exceptions in the later literature are The Perfume Shop (Pirqe de R. Eliezer 25); Paying and Not Paying Tithes (Pesikta de Rab Kahana 10:3); The Wicked and the Righteous in the Inn (Midrash on Ps. 4:13); and Walking in Darkness (27:2, and a variant 119:44).

It is probable that the geminate parables generally reflect the influence of wisdom literature and that ultimately they are the descendants of Psalm 1.

THE ELEMENT OF HUMOR

The gulf between contemporary culture and that of the Rabbis is so great that it is difficult even to guess when their sense of humor paralleled that of today. Did they laugh when we laugh, and vice versa? But some of the parables appeal so strongly to the modern sense of the ridiculous that it is difficult to doubt that they also expected at least a smile from the listeners. Surely no. 40, in which the slave has a choice of eating the rotten fish, enduring a hundred lashes, or paying a heavy fine but ends up enduring part of all three penalties, was told with glee and laughter as it portrayed (caricatured?) the plight of the Egyptians in their dealings with the Israelites. Another case of probable humor is the Parable of the King and the Governor, mentioned in this section, in which the king pushed the governor out of the chariot to make clear to the public which one was king and which one his subordinate. Another is found in the Midrash on Psalms 114:1 (also 105:11), illustrating the reaction of Israelites to Egyptians when the Exodus finally occurred.

> R. Berechiah told a parable of a fat man riding on an ass. The fat man was wondering, "When can I get off the ass?" and the ass was wondering, "When will he get off me?" When the time came for the fat man to get off, I do not know which one was more glad.

Another parable with a strong humorous dimension is found in Esther R. 7:24.

> R. Levi said: The prophecies given to the other nations are ambiguous, and they do not know whether they are to slay or be slain.
> They are like a man who was walking along a road and whose legs began to give way from the hard going. I wish I had an ass, he exclaimed. Soon after a Roman passed by him whose ass had just given birth to a foal and who said to him: Take this foal and ride it. He said: My prayer seems to be heard, but I did not speak properly, (for I did not explain) whether I desired to ride or to carry it. So with the prophecy to the other nations: "That they should be ready against that day" (Est. 3:14): and they did not know whether it was to slay or be slain. But the prophecy to the Jews is clear: "That the Jews should be ready against that day to avenge themselves on their enemies" (8:13).

Still another such parable appears in B. Baba Kamma 60b, virtually identical to a fable in the collection of Babrius. Two students of R. Isaac asked him for instruction, but one insisted on legal points, while the other requested homiletic material.

> He therefore said to them: I will tell you a parable. To what is this like? To a man who has had two wives, one young and one old. The young one used to pluck out his white hair, whereas the old one use to pluck out his black hair. He thus finally remained bald on both sides.

SECULAR PARABLES

While the stories told by the Rabbis were drawn from all facets of their life, the vast majority of the stories were used in relation to the religious tradition that sustained their existence. Even the stories with humor in them were intended to illustrate some aspect of God's past or present dealings with his people or the world. To this generality there are a few apparent exceptions. The parable just quoted from B. Baba Kamma 60b is one of those exceptions and belongs to a small circle of parables that may be labeled "secular," but even in this instance the divergent desires of R. Isaac's two students were related to the Jewish religious tradition.

Of the 125 parables in the present collection nos. 9–11 deal with a father's obligation to teach his son a handicraft and appear to approach the secular model. But in the context of the Tosefta they are an elaboration of the Mishnaic passage dealing with the religious obligations of a father toward his son in the light of the teaching in the Jewish law. They are interpreted to include circumcision, redemption if kidnapped, teaching a trade, marriage, and teaching the regulations of Torah. So the passage is not to be understood simply as prudential advice from a secular booklet "What Every Father Should Know." It is likely that no parable in the present collection can be termed a secular parable. No. 17 at first glance seems to involve the all-too-familiar example of personal antagonism between two leaders, but in the context it proves to reflect the clash between differing interpretations of *halakoth*—that is, the differences between the Schools of Hillel and Shammai.

There are a few instances outside the present collection of parables that may be classified as secular.

> What is the difference between the death of young men and that of old men? R. Judah said: When a lamp goes out of itself, it is good for it and good for the wick; but if it does not go out of itself, it is bad for itself and bad for the wick. R. Abbahu said: When a fig is gathered at the proper time, it is good for itself and good for the tree; but if it is gathered prematurely, it is bad for itself and bad for the tree. (Gen. R. 62:2)

Once R. Abbahu and R. Hiyya b. Abba were both lecturing at the same time. The crowds all went to hear R. Abbahu, who was presenting haggadic material, while R. Hiyya dealt with legal material. When R. Hiyya was disturbed at the disappearance of his audience, R. Abbahu told him the following parable:

> I will give you a parable. To what is the matter like? It is like two men, one of whom was selling precious stones and the other various kinds of small ware. To whom will the people hurry? Is it not to the seller of various kinds of small ware? (B. Sotah 40a)

The talmudic editor reports, however, that despite the parable and the fact that R. Abbahu escorted R. Hiyya home as a sign of personal respect, the latter still was not appeased. Even though the material each was presenting was religious in nature, the tension between the two surely qualified as a secular dispute.

In Ecclesiastes R. 1:18:1 there is a discussion of the phrase "for in much wisdom is much vexation." Subsequent comments interpret this saying to mean that increased learning brings increased responsibility and care, and that the failure of the great is more significant than the failure of the lowly. These remarks are followed by a parable plus proverb-type remarks.

> To what is the matter like? It is like two men who entered a shop. One ate coarse bread and vegetables, while the other ate fine bread and fat meat and drank old wine and partook of an oily sauce and came out feeling ill. The man who had fine food suffered harm, while he who had coarse food escaped harm. Similarly, have you ever seen an ass or camel in convulsions? By whom are pains

experienced? By human beings. R. Ishmael learned: according to the camel is the load.

In B. Kiddushin 59a it is reported that while one Rabbi was negotiating for the purchase of a certain field, another Rabbi bought it. Complaints were made about his actions, and R. Isaac Nappacha took him to task with a story slightly reminiscent of Nathan's story to David (2 Sam. 12:1–4). The parable format is not used, but the story (like Nathan's) forced the Rabbi to convict himself (until he explained that he had acted in innocence).

In Semachoth 14:12 various appropriate responses to a bereaved person are concluded with a parable:

> R. Meir says: He who sees a mourner within the thirty days speaks to him words of consolation and then inquires after his welfare; after thirty days but within twelve months he inquires after his welfare and then speaks to him words of consolation; after twelve months he makes no reference at all (to his bereavement).
>
> R. Meir says: They parable a parable. Unto what is the matter like? It is like one who had a wound and was cured of it, and a physician came and said to him: Pay me a fee, and I will lance your wound and cure you.
>
> Even so is everyone who reminds a mourner after twelve months (of his bereavement): he is accounted as if he had stirred up his wound again.

In addition there are several parables, or sometimes just metaphors, that deal with sexuality, men, and women. See M. Niddah 2:5 and 5:7; Tos. Niddah 2:8 and 3:5; Tos. Zabim 1:11; and B. Kethuboth 10a.

It must be emphasized that while these parables are secular when taken by themselves, they might not have been so regarded by the Rabbis. In fact, they might have been puzzled by the distinction between "secular" and "sacred," since they regarded the whole of life as the area dominated by Torah, that is, the Law, the will of God.

THE RULE OF THREE

It has long been noted that parables tend to develop the story through the use of a triad of persons or events. Thus no. 39, The Escape from Three Perils, recounts the escape of a traveler from a wolf, a lion, and then a serpent; no. 40 tells of the unlucky slave who endured first eating the spoiled fish, then lashes, and finally a fine. In each of these parables the action revolved around the triad; such parables we may say contain major triads. On the other hand, there are parables in which any attentive reader can locate a triad but one that is scarcely essential to the development of the story. In no. 41 the buyer of the field opened up wells and then planted gardens, trees, and orchards in it. This threesome is scarcely a major triad, since it does not shape the basic structure of the story but is added for style or embellishment. Again, no. 52 provides only a minor triad when it narrates that the bridegroom was ashamed sometimes of his bride, sometimes of her immediate family, and sometimes of her more-distant relatives. If the distinction between a major and a minor triad is accepted, then it is likely that only major triads should be accepted as evidence in support of the rule of three.

Unfortunately, opinions will occasionally differ as to whether a triad is major or minor. In view of this element of subjectivity, it may be most helpful to focus attention exclusively on the 125 parables of this collection, on the assumption that they are a sufficiently large collection to be representative. (Certainly they were chosen without any reference to a rule of three or to the distinction between major and minor triads.) A review of the present 125 parables indicates that there are major triads in nos. 8, 39–40, 56, 88(?), 101, and A9. One or two of this group might be questioned by some, but the same reader might replace them with alternatives. This is scarcely a significant percentage of 125 parables, and such significance as it might seem to have is diminished by a comparison with the percentage of parables reflecting what we may call a "rule of two," namely, nos. 2–4, 10, 12, 15, 24, 30, 36, 38, 40, 47, 89, 95–96. Is a parable automatically to be listed under the rule of two when its action hinges on two sons or two daughters or two paths or two administrators and so forth? If the answer is yes, then clearly the parables following a rule of two are more than twice as numerous as those following a rule of three.

Probably it is a mistake to speak of such "rules." The parable in reality is a short-short story. As such it necessarily involves only a limited number of persons, groups, actions, or other items. If comparison or contrast is involved, as is frequently the case, then at least two persons, groups, or actions are necessary. If there is to be a climax, this is often best achieved by adding a third item or even a fourth. But an extension beyond this number clutters the scene and violates the rule of economy. Some parables ignore this last rule, thereby showing its wisdom (e.g., the ten-part parable cited earlier in this chapter). Probably the rule of economy is the dominant principle, and from it results the fact that pairs are more common than triads, and triads more common than quartets.

SERIES OF PARABLES

Occasionally parables are arranged in the rabbinic documents in a series. One Rabbi may tell a parable to illustrate a specific point and then follow it up with a second parable reinforcing the same point. Or a parable told by one Rabbi may be followed by another from a different Rabbi illustrating the same point, an opposite view, or a point only tangentially related to the initial issue. The series that appear in the literature may well reflect the work of the editors rather than an actual sequence of parables told on a single occasion. In some cases parables in a series may come from Rabbis of different generations. Thus nos. 38–39 follow each other immediately in the Mekilta and both illustrate the statement in Jeremiah that the days will come when Israel will no longer refer to the deliverance from Egypt but will speak instead of the deliverance from Babylon (23:7–8). But no. 38 is attributed to Eleazar b. Azariah, a second-generation Tannaim, while no. 39 is attributed to Simeon b. Yohai from the fourth generation of Tannaim.

Similarly nos. 41–42 are brought together in Mekilta because they make the same point about the frustration of the Egyptians when they realized what a treasure they lost through the expulsion of the Hebrews. But the Rabbis involved are from different Tannaitic generations. Nos. 80–82 all illustrate the dictum of R. Akiba that "every section of Scripture is explained by the one that stands next to it." The first of this trio is attributed to R. Akiba himself, and it is left unclear whether the editor assumed the other two are likewise from him or have been added by the editor as further illustrations of R. Akiba's statement.

Nos. 87–88 relate to the same event in Hebrew history (a third parable is part of the series but is not quoted in this collection). No. 3 speaks of learning as a child in contrast with learning as an old man, while no. 4 contrasts learning from a child with learning from an old man. Perhaps they were linked because at first glance they seem to be related. The final comment by Rabbi (i.e., Judah ha-Nasi) was probably intended to warn that while the implications of the previous parables were valid as general principles, one should not absolutize them.

Nos. 9–11 are all attempts to dramatize R. Judah b. Ilai's assertion: "Everyone who does not teach his son a handicraft, teaches him thievery." Nos. 22–23, both by R. Samuel the Younger, were kept together to illustrate his responses to differing answers to prayer for rain. Nos. 26–27 both relate to the fall of Adam and Eve. In the Aboth de R. Nathan there are three parables in sequence dealing with the problem of the "evil inclination" within human life, two of which are quoted in our collection (nos. 32–33).

These are instances of relatively short series of parables, but the later literature provides evidence for more extended series. These were particularly characteristic of homiletic materials such as the Pesikta Rabbati and the Pesikta de Rab Kahana, but also the Midrash on Psalms and Exodus Rabbah. In the Midrash on Psalms 6:3 there are five parables dealing with the opening statement of the psalm, "O Lord, rebuke me not in Thine anger, neither chasten me in Thy wrath." In Exodus R. 20:11–16 (on Exod. 13:17) there are seven parables elaborating the biblical statement, "God led them not by the way of the land of the Philistines," five of them being anonymous, and two attributed to third-century Palestinian Amoraim. In the Pesikta of Rab Kahana (5:11–13) there are eight parables and a parabolic saying on Exodus 12:2, "This month shall be to you a beginning of months," seven of them by named Rabbis, and the eighth attributed to "the Rabbis."

Finally, in the Pesikta Rabbati 11:2 there are some fourteen parables in response to the question, Why is a garden of nuts a symbol of Israel? (a phrase based on Song 6:1). The series begins:

> Because, as R. Joshua of Siknin taught in the name of R. Levi, all other kinds of trees, when sickly, must have earth packed down over their roots in order to recover; but the nut tree, when sickly, must have its roots exposed

if it is to recover. The same is true of Israel: "He that covereth his transgressions shall not prosper; but whoso exposeth them by confessions and forsaketh them shall obtain mercy" (Prov. 28:13).

It must be understood, here and elsewhere, that sometimes the analogies and parables used by the Rabbis were more playful than serious, and priority was given to ingenuity rather than to strict logic.

5

WHAT THE PARABLES MEANT

Our parables were never told merely for their own sake, but always to illustrate, prove, or explain some matter (again, the *Sachhälfte*, or "actuality half"), as distinguished from the story itself (the *Bildhälfte*, or "illustration half"). What the classical rabbinic *mashal* intended to say is seldom in doubt, for it is made clear by both the context and the explicit application, which is attached more often than not. Especially these two features combine to provide what we may call the interpretation of the parable.

Though we say that we are about to make a study of the interpretations of the parables, we must immediately remind ourselves that, from the original rabbinic point of view, that is a backward way of speaking about the matter, for in their contexts the rabbinic parables are intended to be "interpretations" of the matter at hand, whether the latter is a scriptural passage, as is usual, or some other point being established. For the Rabbis the illustration made the actuality more accessible, else it would not have been employed. It is a modern problem that the trope should be looked upon as in need of explanation. Perhaps a unified way of stating the situation is to say that illustration and context are mutually explanatory, and that both together are clearer and more persuasive than either would be alone. Thus that which is elucidated elucidates its elucidation.

It may be recalled that the typical narrative *mashal* in its fullest form consisted of five distinguishable parts. It is with the first and fourth parts—the illustrand and the application—that we are concerned in this chapter. Normally it is to be expected that the illustrand and the application will be consonant with each other, and where a disjunction or serious dissonance between them occurs, the possibility of there having been a reapplication of the parable and its imperfect assimilation to a new context must be considered.

THE ILLUSTRAND

The matter to be illustrated is logically prior to the illustration. This fact can be seen clearly in a number of ways. For example, in some cases the parable is explicitly adduced to resolve a perplexity presented by Scripture. In an anonymous parable in Sifre on Numbers 84, this feature is especially clear.

> "And Moses said: Rise up, O Lord" (Num. 10:35). One Scripture says: "According to the command of the Lord they remained in camp, and according to the command of the Lord they set out" (9:20). But another Scripture [10:35] says that they broke camp at the command of Moses. How can these two passages be reconciled?
>
> A parable. It is like unto a king of flesh and blood who said to his servant: Please be so good as to remind me to be on my way because I go to obtain an inheritance for my son.

Obviously the parable is intended to explain the illustrand, not the reverse. This fact is also demonstrated by instances in which context takes priority over convention, as in The Proud Father (no. 38). As we will see, the metaphor of the father is conventionally used in most parables to represent God, and son or daughter usually represents Israel. But in this parable the matter to be illustrated demands that the father represent Israel, and the daughter and son represent deliverances from Egypt and from Babylon. Clearly the story is subordinate to the illustrand.

It is understood, then, that we speak of "interpretations of the parables" only as an accommodation to the concerns of the modern student, for whom the meanings of the parables appear problematic. This is not to say, however, that the parables would have been transparent to their ancient hearers if they had been divorced from the contexts in which they were used, or that they needed no explanation when first uttered. Certainly, a parable such as no. 36, which distressingly lacks an explicit application, requires of us today no little guesswork about its precise interpretation. Presumably the original audience had more to go by. But in some instances even contemporaries were puzzled; we have examples of parables of which the parabling Rabbi was requested by his disciples to provide an explanation, or of which Rabbis gave private explanations to their disciples that differed from those given to outsiders (see the rabbinic references in David Daube, "Public Pronouncement and Private Explanation in the Gospels," *Expository Times* 62 [1945–46]: 175–77).

The importance of the illustrand as an indicator of the meaning of the parable is greatest in those items that lack explicit applications following them—about 20 percent of our total number of items.

THE APPLICATION

The great majority of rabbinic parables (nearly 80 percent) have as one of their features an explicit interpretation of the story, usually following it. This we may call the application, the fourth part of the typical parabolic unit. G. V. Jones (*The Art and Truth of the Parables* [London: SPCK, 1964], p. 59) suggests the term *epignome* for this feature.

This phenomenon belies the modern idea that an effective illustration, like a good joke, needs no explanation, and that hence a good parable will have no such thing. Strange as it may seem, this phenomenon is found even for parables that would seem to have been perfectly understandable apart from such a feature. It is part of the normal pattern. On the other hand, we do notice a faintly perceptible tendency for the number of parables without this feature to be fewer in the earlier parables—those from the earlier generations of Tannaim and those in Mishnah and Tosefta, but also in the Babylonian Talmud. Items ascribed to the first generation of Tannaim, however, do not conform to that pattern (about 64 percent of their parables have applications), and neither do the so-called Tannaitic *midrashim*, Sifra, Sifre).

The application is normally linked to the story by a verbal hinge. By far the most common linking word is the single Hebrew word *kak*. Sometimes it is combined with other words. For example, in a number of cases we find *aph kak* (also likewise), as in no. 8. *Aph* alone is sometimes found, as in nos. 25 and 103. In a number of cases the application makes a contrast with the situation pictured in the parable, and then the natural linking word is *ebal* (but), as in no. 50. Other linking words are "therefore" (no. 79), "behold" (no. 58), "accordingly," and a few other phrases.

There is considerable variety of structure and form to be seen among the applications attached to the Tannaitic parables. Quite common is a simple statement, explaining the meaning or expressing the purpose of the parable without proof texts or any special rhetorical features, as in the application of The Escape from Three Perils (no. 39): "Even so is Israel. Later troubles cause the former ones to be forgotten." Sometimes it is a point-by-point explanation of the parable—what Jülicher would have called an allegorizing interpretation (as in nos. 56, 69, and 78). Another type of application consists of the simple citation of Scripture with no other explanation, generally introduced by the formula "as it is said" or "for it is said" (as in no. 54). A combination of the simple type and the scriptural type produces a third, which may be called compound applications—or better, using the terminology of syntax, complex applications, for the scriptural component is usually subordinate to the statement component. Normally the explanatory statement comes first and is then clinched by one or more proof texts. About 22 percent of the Tannaitic parables have such applications (e.g., no. 37). A variation has statement and scriptural quotation altering at least twice, as in no. 44. There are other less common types, but it would be tedious to list them all.

Since the Rabbis evidently felt no obligation to conform to Aristotelian canons defining parable or allegory, it is not surprising to find that there is sometimes a rather imperfect parallel between application and parable. In no. 112, for example, the parable mentions only the mother, but the application mentions both father and mother. In no. 85 the application does not closely match the parable, resulting in a certain opaqueness of the item.

We noted that in 1886 Jülicher laid down a rule that subsequently was widely accepted by students of the parables: a true parable has only one point of comparison (the tertium comparationis) between the actuality half and the illustration half of the parable. If there are more, the item is an allegory, and there is no such thing as a mixture of allegory and parable. C. H. Dodd adopted this law from Jülicher and declared that "the parables [of Jesus] could have been taken for allegorical mystifications only in a non-Jewish environment" (*The Parables of the Kingdom* [New York: Charles Scribner's Sons, 1961], p. 4). But the ancient Rabbis, never having heard of Jülicher or Dodd, made no effort to conform to their decrees.

Not only do the majority of rabbinic parables have attached applications, but those applications frequently interpret the stories point by point; or again, they often attach meaning to some but not all the features of the story. In short, the narrative *mashal* draws no boundary whatever along the lines of Jülicher's bifurcation of "parable" and "allegory."

It may be possible to assert simultaneously that a parable has but one main point and that yet specific figures within it have significations of their own, if it can be maintained that there are both primary and secondary tertia comparationis. A parable would then have at least two levels of interpretation: the meaning of individual figures within the parable, and the meaning of the parable as a whole. Minimum interpretation would be limited to the latter, while maximum interpretation would embrace also the former. Thus in the trio of parables, nos. 9–11, the main point could be expressed in the imperative: "Teach your son a skill!" But the actual form of the parables is indicative, and the application, which is not here explicit, but clear enough, might be thus expressed: A man with a craft is secure like a vineyard with a fence, and like a vine branch protected by an enclosure: while a man without a craft is vulnerable like an unfenced vineyard, the prey of beasts and all who pass by. Also, a man with a craft is secure like a married woman, who has nothing to fear from men; while a man without a craft is like an unmarried woman, vulnerable to any impudent man. The main point could therefore be expressed in the indicative: A skilled man is secure, but an unskilled man is vulnerable. This is the primary tertium comparationis. But this lesson could not be derived if the individual figures were impenetrable. The woman, for example, represents a man, her husband is a man's craft, and the aggressive men are economic dangers. These are the secondary tertia comparationis, and one could not arrive at the primary one if one did not instinctively understand the secondary ones, which are self-evident. But there is a remainder: Not every feature can be matched up with something in the illustrand, nor do all carry metaphoric weight.

While in many items the distinction between primary and secondary seems easy enough to make, in many others it is not so easy to decide what is primary and what is secondary, nor is it easy to determine the number of each, and we begin to wonder if we are imposing something alien upon the parable in view. This problem must be kept in mind when we begin trying to count how many points of comparison there are in each item.

Sometimes there is clearly only one primary point, as in the application of no. 39, which is simple and unitary. In it the existence of secondary tertia cannot reasonably be denied: The traveler is Israel, and the encounters with dangerous beasts are Israel's troubles and deliverances. But these secondary points are entirely subordinate to the primary point. A number of other such examples could be cited, but the number of more questionable items is greater, in which the unitary nature of the application depends largely on the eye of the beholder. Nevertheless, with due warning that such judgment is often unavoidably subjective, it can be said that the great majority of our items appear to have but one primary tertium comparationis.

There is a smaller number of items in which it does not seem possible to reduce the number of primary tertia comparationis to only one without doing violence to the actuality half, especially as embodied in the application. Thus in no. 37 there seems no way to find any less than two primary tertia, if we are not to ignore the explicit application: There is Jonah's flight from God, and God's apprehension of Jonah; mentioning these two is to speak nothing of secondary tertia comparationis, for there seem to be at least four obvious metaphors. About 20 percent of our 325 items belong in such a category, while a few others have three (such as no. 44) or even four (no. 46) primary points of comparison.

To speak of secondary tertia comparationis, referring to figures within the parable that seem to carry obvious metaphoric weight of their own, is to raise the bugbear of allegory and allegorization, but we must not be afraid to see what we see. Some items are almost pure allegories, as Jülicher defined allegory, for their attached applications interpret them as such. What else can we call The Lame and Blind Caretakers (no. 49)? But the majority of items contain some figures that correspond to features in the interpretation and other features that cannot without strain find any such correspondence, or there are elements in the interpretation that are not figured forth in the story. Thus in no. 37 there is nothing in the story that corresponds to the Gentiles referred to in the application. Similar remainders are left over, either in the interpretation or in the story, in nos. 45, 57, 62, 86, and others.

STANDARD METAPHORS

There is a large category of rabbinic metaphors used in the *meshalim* that we may call "standard metaphors." They are to be distinguished from other metaphors in that they fairly consistently carry the same freight, so that their translation into literal terms is generally predictable. The "decoding" of such metaphors is virtually automatic, a very simple operation for persons who were cultured in the metaphor repertoire. Many of these metaphors had biblical roots.

We could compile a lexicon of these metaphors, the most frequent of which is that of the *king*, usually representing God, as was discussed in chapter 4. Likewise a *father* usually stood for God (as in no. 44), but in no. 38 he is Israel, and in no. 76 he is Moses. God may also be represented in the parables as a *master* of servants and slaves, a *proprietor* or *householder* (cf. no. 70), a *husband* (no. 65), or a *depositary* (no. 106). We also encounter the *son*, who is usually Israel (no. 44), but *sons* may also be individual tribes of Israel (no. 47). *Daughter* is less consistent in meaning but often also represents Israel; she can also be Torah or wisdom. Daughter and son are used in a special way in no. 38. When the husband is

God, the *wife* is Israel (no. 52), a metaphor with deep biblical roots.

Ancient marriages required the services of a go-between agent to make arrangements, or a *groomsman;* in our parables he is usually Moses (no. 28). The *slave* appears frequently in singular or plural, but the significance varies: Israel or the pious within Israel (no. 94), the gentile nations in general or perhaps Egypt (no. 40), Moses (no. 89), angels, elements of nature, or named individuals. In addition to having slaves or servants, one might employ day laborers or other *employees,* which can be Israelites or heathen. The king may have a *friend,* who is usually Israel, but sometimes Moses. The *tutor* often appears and nearly always represents Moses (no. 52), but in no. 114 he is Jeremiah, and in no. 77 he may be the chastising angels. That the tutor could represent either Moses or angels recalls that both are closely associated in the Sinai episode, according to Galatians 3:19–20. The *steward* is sometimes interchangeable with the tutor and has the same meanings. Another intermediary role is that of the *orator-advocate* (no. 102), who is Moses representing his client, Israel.

Other metaphors are less frequent, and some are clearly ad hoc. To the degree that they were customary, however, they could be readily decoded by the audience, making the interpretation of the parables all the more obvious.

6

THE USE OF SCRIPTURE IN RABBINIC PARABLES

Even a casual reader of rabbinic parables notes the extensive role played by Scripture in these parables. This orientation is not surprising, since the basic purpose of rabbinic literature—including the parables—was to affirm, interpret, glorify, and apply the words of the Jewish Scriptures to the contemporary life of the believing community. For convenience, we may divide the role of Scripture in connection with the parables into three areas. First, Scripture may be *in the illustrand*, the introductory part of the parable establishing, at least in some broad sense, the point to be illustrated. Second, Scripture may be *in the story half*. Finally, Scripture may be *in the attached interpretation*. The majority of parables have interpretations attached to them even when the illustrand may have provided the clue necessary for the application of the story. Illustrand and interpretation serve a similar purpose, but the interpretation following the parable is frequently more detailed than the illustrand. The illustrand raises the issue, the story responds to that issue, and the interpretation develops in detail how the story speaks to the issue.

SCRIPTURE IN THE ILLUSTRAND

In the present collection of parables an effort has been made to include enough of the material immediately preceding a parable to provide a sense of the direction of the parable. A review of the 125 parables of this collection indicates that in roughly four out of five cases the illustrand relates to a passage of Scripture: it contains either a quotation from Scripture or, in some cases, an issue that emerges from a Scripture passage. Of the remaining 20 percent of the parables, some have no illustrand, and some, while raising theological issues, do not deal directly with matters taken from the Jewish Scriptures. Thus no. 106 deals with the death of the wicked and the righteous, but the discussion does not relate to a specific passage of Scripture. In fact, there is a distinctive group of parables that are from the sphere of Jewish religion and ethics but constitute a kind of subform within the category of rabbinic parables. They all deal with a class or type of person, differ somewhat in their introductory structure from the other parables, and normally are a double parable contrasting two types of persons. See nos. 2–4, 10–11, 24, 30, and 49. They are closer to the wisdom literature than to the mainstream of Hebrew-Jewish Scriptures. They are not responses to specific passages in the Jewish Scriptures, although many relate indirectly to issues involved in those Scriptures.

Understandably the rabbinic documents with the highest proportion of illustrands taken from the Scriptures are those that are basically commentaries on Scripture, for example, the Mekilta on Exodus, Sifra on Leviticus, Sifre on Numbers and Deuteronomy, and the Midrash Rabbah. On the other hand, the percentage shifts the other way in the Mishnah, Tosefta, Babylonian Talmud, and the Aboth de Rabbi Nathan. In our file of 1,500 parables more than two-thirds of the parables that have illustrands include Scripture quotations or issues raised by Scripture passages.

Parables relate in various ways to the Scripture cited or alluded to in their illustrands. While it is impossible to draw a hard and fast line between the various patterns, most of the parables serve one or more of the following five functions in connection with the Scripture indicated in the illustrand:

1. Simply illustrate a text, without adding any new information.
2. Beautify or adorn a text or make it more impressive.
3. Expand or clarify a text.
4. Defend or justify a text or a teaching from a text.
5. Harmonize one text with another or with accepted teaching.

Most parables involve at least two of these functions, and opinions will differ as to which function is primary and which secondary. Thus a parable whose primary function is to illustrate a passage of Scripture serves almost inevitably to beautify it or make it more impressive.

A considerable number of parables illustrate the text of the illustrand without adding any significant information to that already contained in the text itself. Parables may be placed in this category if the reader returns a negative answer to the question: Does the parable go beyond the text in any significant way? Parable no. 28 could be classified in this group. The behavior of Moses in breaking the tablets containing the Ten Commandments when he found the people involved in idolatry is compared with the action of the king's agent who destroyed the betrothal agreement when the bride-to-be was discovered to be unworthy. On second thought, however, the parable may go beyond or even change the biblical record. In the Scriptures it appears that Moses broke the tablets out of anger against the people, while in the parable the allegedly analogous action was performed as an act of mercy to protect the bride (i.e., the people of Israel) from the worst consequences of her behavior.

Perhaps no. 92 provides a better example of a parable in which the Scripture text is merely illustrated. The quotation is from Deuteronomy 11:17 and warns that if the Israelites do not follow the divine command, the anger of the Lord will descend upon them. The illustration adds little to this verse when it reports that the king's son who failed to follow his father's instructions at the banquet was humiliated and thrown out of the palace. (One may question whether a prince would be treated in this fashion, but the point is clear, and its meaning strictly parallel to the Scripture text.) Again, no. 84 speaks of the Moabites and Midianites, who combined against Israel despite their previous enmity to each other.

This is illustrated by the analogy of quarreling dogs that unite against an attacking wolf. No new information is provided about Moabites or Midianites or their antagonism for each other and for Israel. See also no. 13.

Other parables illustrate a Scripture passage but also go beyond the text itself by way of explanation or clarification. For example, no. 101 deals with the text "for the Lord's portion is His people" (Deut. 32:9). The parable develops a complicated historical background explaining this statement. The precise meaning of the details is not clear until the interpretation is added, but the parable plus interpretation reflects the clashes between the descendants of Isaac and Jacob on the one side and those of Ishmael, Keturah, and Esau on the other. Probably a further function of the parable is to defend and justify the special position of Israel over against the other biological descendants of Abraham. It may be debated which function is primary, but clearly the parable goes beyond the text in Deuteronomy.

It has already been stated that any parable associated with a Scripture passage tends to focus attention on the passage and thus to hallow or beautify it in the minds of the hearers or readers. Parables that may have had as a primary purpose the beautifying or adorning of a Scripture teaching are parables that strike the reader as being particularly apt or illuminating—though it is impossible to be certain that the responses of the original readers corresponded with those of today. No. 109 is a striking parable as it tells of the villager who inadvertently smashed a whole basket of valuable glassware by a careless motion of his staff. The proprietor then shows him all that has been destroyed, saying, "I know that I cannot obtain redress from you, but come and I will show you how much valuable stuff you have destroyed." The interpretation explains that this story illumines Genesis 3:7 ("and the eyes of them both were opened"); that is, God made Adam and Eve see how much destruction they had occasioned by their violation of God's command.

Again, no. A1 is a particularly moving parable. It is the story of a widow and her two sons who searched in vain for food because the farmers had ignored the biblical injunctions about the gleanings, the forgotten sheaf, the corners of the field, and the tithe for the poor. This example parable was intended primarily for its ethical effect with its dramatic and powerful affirmation of the biblical concern for the poor and needy. The result is to beautify and adorn the Scripture regulations—not art for art's sake but rather art for ethics' sake!

Probably nos. 27 and 44 could also be cited as parables intended to beautify and adorn a Scripture passage. Genesis R. 12:15 presents another parable in this category.

> . . . "The Lord God [made earth and heaven]" (Gen. 1:1). This may be compared to a king who had some empty glasses. Said the king: If I pour hot water into them, they will burst; if cold, they will contract [and snap]. What then did the king do? He mixed hot and cold water and poured it into them, and so they remained [unbroken].
>
> Even so, said the Holy One, blessed be He: If I create the world on the basis of mercy alone, its sins will be great; on the basis of judgment alone, the world cannot exist. Hence I will create it on the basis of judgment and of mercy, and may it then stand! Hence the expression, "The Lord God."
>
> [In Jewish tradition the Hebrew term translated "Lord" was thought to present God in his character of mercy, while the term translated "God" represented him as the God of judgment].

It should be clear that suggesting which parables had as a major purpose the adorning or beautifying of a given Scripture involves a subjective judgment. But certainly this was a significant function of the parables, even though there may be disagreements as to when such a function played a major role in the thought of the Rabbis.

No. 37 is a good illustration of a parable intended to harmonize a Scripture statement with accepted theological views. The tractate Pischa in Mekilta begins with Exodus 12:1, "And the Lord spake unto Moses and Aaron in the land of Egypt." Then follows a discussion of the Lord's speaking both to Moses and to Aaron. In Pischa 1:35 attention shifts to the final phrase, "in the land of Egypt." This created a problem, since it was a dictum of Jewish thought that God revealed himself only in the land of Israel. This principle is explicitly recognized here as follows:

> Before the land of Israel had been especially chosen, all lands were suitable for divine revelation; after the land of Israel had been chosen, all other lands were eliminated. Before Jerusalem had been especially selected, the entire land of Israel was suitable for altars; after Jerusalem had

been selected, all the rest of the land in Israel was eliminated. . . . Before the temple had been especially selected, the whole of Jerusalem was appropriate for the manifestation of the divine presence; after the temple had been selected, the rest of Jerusalem was eliminated. (Mek. Pischa 1:42–49).

But there were obvious exceptions to the general principle enunciated here. There follows a discussion about these exceptions, and the experience of Jonah is mentioned ("But Jonah rose up to flee unto Tarshish from the presence of the Lord," Jonah 1:3), and the parable is then narrated to indicate how false Jonah's expectation was that he could escape from the divine presence simply by fleeing the land of Israel.

Again, no. 14 deals with the problem created by the fact that according to the biblical tradition God himself wrote on the first tablets, while the tables that replaced them were prepared by Moses. The analogy given is that the king himself would provide the documents of betrothal when becoming engaged to a woman, but—according to the parable story—the woman would have to provide the necessary materials in the event of a divorce. This analogy is less than entirely satisfactory, since in the case of the second tablets Moses was not the offending party and the documents were not intended for a divorce but a renewed contract. The story is valid in the sense that it illustrates that different circumstances call for different procedures. Apparently the rabbinic tradition itself recognized the inadequacies of this version of the parable, since the revised version in Deuteronomy R. 3:17, although still attributed to Johanan b. Zakkai, is expanded and reports that the second set of documents was prepared not for a divorce but for a reconciliation. Again, no. 21 harmonizes two verses of Scripture about lifting up the countenance by explaining that the two texts refer to two different situations and so are not really contradictory.

There may well be other ways in which parables function in relation to the Scriptures in the illustrands, but at least these five can be identified—however much opinions may differ with respect to the classification of individual parables.

SCRIPTURE IN THE STORY HALF

In view of the extensive use of Scripture in the illustrands, it may be surprising that there is negligible evidence
of the introduction of Scripture into the story half of the
rabbinic parables. In the present collection only no. 76
appears to introduce a Scripture reference into the parable
story. And even this reference to the Jeremiah passage reads
like an afterthought added at the end of the incident by some
editor who was reminded by the story of the tragic fate of
King Zedekiah, whose sons were executed before his eyes.
In the larger repertory of rabbinic parables there are a few
instances in which Scripture quotations or near-quotations
seem to appear in the story half of a parable, but in most
cases it turns out that these phrases are actually part of the
illustrand or the interpretation.

Consider the Pesikta de Rab Kahana 27:9:

> In another comment the verse is read "Take for your own
> sake . . . [a cluster including] the fruit of goodly trees"
> etc. (Lev. 23:40), "the fruit of goodly trees" [the ethrog]
> standing for [a kind of men in] Israel: even as the ethrog
> has aroma and has edible fruit, so Israel have men in their
> own midst who have knowledge of Torah and also have
> the merit of good deeds. "And branches of palm trees"
> (ibid.) also stand for [a kind of men in] Israel: as the palm
> tree has edible fruit but no aroma, so Israel have men in
> their midst who have knowledge of Torah but do not have
> the merit of good deeds. "And branches of a tree screened
> by its network of foliage" (ibid.) also stand for [a kind of
> men in] Israel: as the myrtle tree has aroma but does not
> have edible fruit, so Israel have men in their midst who
> have the merit of good deeds but do not have Torah.
> "And willows of the brook" (ibid.) also stand for [a kind
> of men in] Israel: even as the willow has neither edible
> fruit nor aroma, so Israel have men in their midst in
> whom there is neither knowledge of Torah nor the merit
> of good deeds.

While Scripture is deeply woven into the fabric of this text,
upon analysis it is evident that this is not a single parable (if
that term is appropriate at all) but rather a series of what may
be called "parablettes." Each parablette consists of three
parts: (1) a phrase of Scripture that functions as an illustrand; (2) an item from the field of dendrology (ethrog,

palm, myrtle, willow); and (3), the comparison or interpretation applying characteristics of the tree to types of persons in Israel.

In Genesis R. 38:2 there is a parable that does indeed include a quotation from Scripture as part of the story.

> R. Abba b. Kahana began thus: "Thus thou shouldest bray a fool in a mortar with a pestle among groats" etc. (Prov. 27:22). Said R. Abba b. Kahana: Like a man who pounds barley in a frame, so he [who chastises the fool] thinks to improve him, yet even as it [the pestle] rises and falls, "Yet will his foolishness not depart from him" (ibid.). Thus the generation of the Flood was removed from the generation of separation, but "two years after the Flood" (Gen. 11:10), yet, "and the whole earth was of one language" etc. (v. 1).

Again, in Numbers R. 2:15 there is a parable story in which language from Hosea 1–2 appears in the statement of the king about his wife: "I will divorce her and have no pity on her children. She is not my wife and I am not her husband." In Midrash on Psalms 73:4 there is a parable attributed to R. Samuel b. Nachmani in which the story half concludes with an explicit quotation from Jeremiah 31:22, and the story is then compared to the relation between God and Israel in this world and in the world to come. There is a parable in the Pirqe de Rabbi Eliezer 34 attributed to Rabbi Zechariah in which the story half concludes with a quotation from Job 33:15–16, and then the whole is compared to death and the awakening beyond. There is an intriguing narrative in Song R. 2:2:4 where R. Hanan of Sepphoris describes three different situations in each of which ten men were present but none was able to recite the appropriate blessing. Then another man appeared and repeated the blessing. After each incident the question is asked: To what is the matter/he like? and in each case the same answer given: a "rose among thorns" (Song 2:2). In a sense the interpretation comes first in these three incidents, then the rhetorical question, and then the abbreviated story (i.e., the Scripture quotation).

Apart from these rare exceptions, however, Scripture quotations are not normally a part of the story half of the rabbinic parables.

SCRIPTURE IN THE ATTACHED INTERPRETATIONS

If the use of Scripture is rare in the story half of rabbinic parables, the reverse is the case in the interpretations so frequently attached to such stories. In Johnston's collection of 325 parables some 60 percent of the parables that have interpretations attached include one or more Scripture quotations in those interpretations. The percentage is slightly lower for the 125 parables in part 1. But when the file of some 1,500 items is reviewed, the percentage of parables with attached interpretations that include Scripture quotations is just over 75 percent. On the average the parables from the later period are higher in Scripture quotations than those from the earlier period. Thus if one deducts from the 1,500 items the 325, apparently early, parables of Johnston's dissertation, the percentage of attached interpretations with Scripture in the remaining nearly 1,200 rises to 80 percent. Perhaps it should be repeated that all of these statistics exclude the minority of parables that lack any attached interpretations.

A review of the documents involved shows that the high percentage just mentioned is due chiefly to the high percentage of Scripture quotations in the Midrash Rabbah on the five books of Moses and the five Megilloth (Lamentations, Ruth, Ecclesiastes, Esther, and the Song of Solomon). In the group just mentioned, Genesis Rabbah has the lowest percentage and presumably is the earliest in its date of origin. In addition, the Midrash on Psalms also provides an extraordinarily high proportion of interpretations including Scripture.

It may be of interest to examine the ways in which the Scripture quotations function in the interpretations. The simplest, and certainly one of the most common, patterns is created when there is a Scripture passage in the illustrand that is then repeated in the interpretation. Thus the parable is sandwiched between the introductory use of a Scripture text in the illustrand and its repetition in the interpretation. For examples, see nos. 15, 20, 50, 59, 63, 65, and others.

In another group of parables the Scripture in the interpretation does not repeat the quotation in the illustrand but is one that has been suggested by, or that illuminates, some aspect of the parable story. In no. 100 the illustrand quotes Deuteronomy 32:5, which identifies Israel as "a

generation perverse and perverted." The story then describes how a crooked rod must sometimes be heated in the
fire and then pounded if it is to be made straight. The
quotation in the interpretation picks up this image of the rod
straightened by fire and beating and cites Ezekiel 21:31,
"And I will deliver you into the hand of brutal men, forgers
[or, smiths] of destruction." The latter quotation is made
relevant not by the illustrand but by the metaphorical
language of the parable story. In no. 102 the illustrand uses
the phrase "he found him in a desert land" (Deut. 32:10) to
describe Abraham. The story then describes the deliverance
of the king from the desert by "a certain brave man." The
Scripture in the interpretation relates this event to God's
leading Abraham from Ur of the Chaldees into the Promised
Land (Gen. 15:7). The conclusion carries the story beyond
the initial statement in the illustrand, although this conclusion was present also in the unquoted verses in Deuteronomy 32. Nos. 19 and 107–8 also illustrate this usage.

In another set of parables there is no Scripture quotation
in the illustrand, and sometimes no real illustrand at all, but
the message of the story is expressed or reinforced by the
Scripture quoted in the interpretation. Thus in no. 2 there is
no formal illustrand, but the point of each half of the double
parable story is made explicit and authoritative by the
attached Scripture. Actually, if the Scripture had been
quoted first in the illustrand, the imagery of the parable
would have lost some of its force, that is, it would have been
a rather weak imitation of the Scripture. As noted, this is a
geminate or twin parable, and generally these do not have
illustrands. In no. 18 what functions as an illustrand
provides information about the historical situation in which
R. Akiba ignored the Roman regulation prohibiting the study
or practice of Jewish law. Then the parable is his response to
the complaints of his coreligionists that he was endangering
his life by his actions. After telling this parable (fable),
R. Akiba brought home the point of the story with the
assertion that for the Jewish community the very essence of
its life was in the study of Torah and the service of God. The
Scripture quotation in the interpretation is the punch line
from Deuteronomy 30:20, "For that is thy life and the length
of thy days." Other illustrations of this pattern are nos. 2, 24,
27, 33, and 36.

Most of the parables cited so far have generally only one

Scripture quotation in the interpretation, but the situation becomes more complicated when there are a number of different quotations linked together. They may not all function in the same way. In general, however, they reaffirm the motif of the illustrand or develop the thought beyond a Scripture already quoted—sometimes because the story of the parable has provided a new angle of thought. For multiple Scripture quotations in the interpretations, see nos. 53, 101, 103, and 112.

7

THE RECYCLING
OF PARABLES

A matter of considerable interest, especially because of its bearing on the study of the parables of Jesus, is the problem of determining to what extent the rabbinic literature preserves the original contexts and retains the original meanings of the parables, and to what extent these stories have been "recycled" and used for new purposes. A related question is the extent to which they could be transformed or modified.

Every parable has a life history that may begin before birth. Many a parable is but one stage in a process of repeated transformation. Thus The Escape from Three Perils (no. 39) clearly is developed from the simile in Amos 5:19 ("As if a man fled from a lion, and a bear met him; or went into the house and leaned with his hand against the wall, and a serpent bit him"). The Well-Rooted Tree (no. 2) was doubtless suggested by Jeremiah 17:6, 8, which in fact most manuscripts of the Mishnah incorporate into the parable. These, like many of the parables, grow directly out of biblical pictures, so that the parables themselves are already a recycling of older material.

THE ORIGINALITY OF INTERPRETATIONS

Many of the parables were obviously created to accompany the illustrands with which we now find them occurring, for their content is clearly determined by their illustrands. Thus no. 46 is transparently worked out under the influence of Psalm 114, which is assumed by the illustrand to be an expansion of Exodus 14:21, which is being commented upon. Likewise no. 67 is plainly patterned after Leviticus 18:28, with which the illustrand deals. We must interpret nos. 38–39 in the light of the text in Jeremiah that they were palpably manufactured to illustrate. We may be confident in all such cases that we have essentially the original context of the parables.

The majority of our parables are related to their contexts in such a way that even in that minority of cases in which there is no attached application, their meanings in general or in detail can be inferred with some degree of certainty. So close is the correspondence between some parables and their illustrands that we can be sure we have their original settings, and we can in fact see through the process by which they were composed, so transparent is their tropic transformation of the literal point.

In the light of the conventional wisdom that a good parable does not need to be explained, the question may be properly raised whether the explanatory applications usually found attached to our parables were originally part of the parabolic pericope, or whether they are secondary accretions. That many of these explicit applications must have originated together with the parables to which they remain attached can be demonstrated by a number of striking cases. Thus in no. 64 there is something incongruous about either a princess or a queen performing household duties, as the parable has it. The figures are chosen so as not to compromise the dignity of Aaron and Moses, and female figures are chosen to represent the nature of the activities required. The parable had to be manufactured to fit the lesson that is expressed in the application. The illustration story, while having a life of its own, has been accommodated to the illustrand. (Flusser calls this compromise between realism and illustrative function *Verfremdung*, "strangification.")

Again, in nos. 67–69 the parables so minutely anticipate the applications that we must recognize the connections between them to have existed from the beginning; the total pericopes form primitive units. In no. 48 the close and detailed correspondence between parable and application suggests that both must have been created together. In such cases, of which the reader of our examples in part 1 will have noticed many, it is inconceivable that the parable could have existed before the application, since in so many of them the details have been obviously manipulated, even to the point of creating awkwardness or implausibility within the story, in order to make it correspond closely to the application. On the other hand, it is unlikely that the application could have existed before the parable, for an apodosis is inconceivable without a protasis; applications, in contrast to illustrands, can hardly have an independent existence.

This is not to say that in the mind of the parabler the points in the application may not have arisen before the parable that he made to support it or prepare for it. In an elaborate parable attributed to Jose b. Halafta (first half of the second century) in Pesikta de Rab Kahana 1:3, the application may be in some sense, perhaps psychological, chronologically prior to the parable to which it is attached; but it could hardly have arisen later.

> "Even upon the crown wherewith his mother hath crowned him in the day of his espousals" (Song 3:11). R. Isaac said: We searched through all of Scripture, from first to last, and did not find that Bathsheba made a crown for Solomon; but this means the Tent of Meeting, which is (like a crown) topped with blue, purple, and scarlet.
>
> R. Hunya said: R. Simeon b. Yohai asked R. Eleazar bar R. Jose: Have you perhaps heard from your father [R. Jose b. Halafta] an interpretation of the verse "even upon the crown wherewith his mother hath crowned him"?
>
> He said to him: It is like a king who had a daughter whom he loved inordinately. He did not stop calling her endearing names until he had called her "my sister"; he did not stop calling her endearing names until he had called her "my mother."
>
> Even so, at the beginning, the Holy One, blessed be He, loved Israel and called her "My daughter"—"Hearken, O daughter, and consider" (Ps. 45:10). He did not stop calling her endearing names until He called her "My sister"—"My sister, my bride" (Song 5:1). He did not stop calling her endearing names until He called her "My mother"—as it is said: "Attend unto Me, O My people,

and give ear unto Me, O My nation" (Isa. 51:4), where
u-le-'ummi (My nation) is spelled defectively so that it may
be read u-le-'immi (My mother).

R. Simeon b. Yohai arose, kissed R. Eleazar on the
brow, and said to him: Had I come and heard nothing but
this interpretation, I would have been content. (Pĕsikta dĕ-
Rab Kahăna. Translated by William G. Braude and Israel J.
Kapstein [Philadelphia: Jewish Publication Society, 1975],
pp. 10–11.)

If we think of the meaning as a whole, including the
illustrand, it is very common to observe a conscious effort to
make the parable fit into its role within the pericope, even at
the risk of awkwardness and artificiality.

In any case, in the marriage of parable with application,
the latter is generally the dominant partner and would not
normally be secondary. If anything, when earlier and later
versions of a parable have survived, it can sometimes be seen
that there is a progressive tendency to enhance the parallelism between parable and application, usually by elaborating
the parable. This can be seen, for example, by comparing no.
43 with its later version in Song R. 2:14:2.

> It was taught in the School of R. Ishmael: When Israel
> went forth from Egypt, unto what were they like? They
> were like unto a dove that fled from a hawk and flew into
> the cleft of a rock and found a serpent lurking there.
> When it tried to get right in, it could not, because the
> serpent was lurking there; and when it tried to turn back,
> it could not, because the hawk was hovering outside.
> What then did the dove do? It began to cry and beat its
> wings so that the owner of the cote should hear and come
> to its rescue.
>
> Even so was Israel like this at the sea. They could not
> go down into the sea, because it had not yet been divided
> before them. They could not turn back, because Pharaoh
> had already drawn near. What did they do? "And they
> were sore afraid; and the children of Israel cried out unto
> the Lord" (Exod. 14:10). Then straightway: "Thus the
> Lord saved Israel that day" (v. 30).

There is a yet more extensively elaborated version in Exodus
R. 20:6, where the parable is thoroughly allegorized.

It appears that parable and application often circulated
together as a unit, as seen in the case of The Escape from
Three Perils (no. 39), which occurs several times and always

with exactly the same application—to the very word—
though the illustrand may vary somewhat.

The conclusion to which all this points ought not to be
surprising. The rabbinic parables at their genesis normally
included an explicit application. This feature was common in
the earlier period and became all but obligatory in later
periods, in harmony with the general trend of rabbinic
parables to become more and more formally stereotyped. But
parable and application could be divorced and new matings
produced, especially when there was reapplication of the
parables to a new or different point. To such cases we now
turn.

THE REAPPLICATION OF PARABLES

An effective parable, like a powerful proof text, might be
invoked in more than one context, for it is a hammer that can
drive in more than one nail. Or, to change the figure, a good
illustration is like a nail from which more than one picture
can be hung.

There are some four kinds of indications that a parable
has received a new application. In ascending order of
objectivity and certainty (the last two being almost equally
certain), they are (1) indications within the parable itself or
its context, such as maladjustment or imperfect assimilation
to its present context; (2) apparent disjunction between the
illustrand and the application; (3) cases in which the parable
is positively known to derive from a story used in an alien
source, such as an Aesopic fable or Greek myth; and
(4) cases in which parallel versions of the same parable have
different applications.

Suspicion of reapplication to a context other than the
original one that gave birth to the parable may be warranted
when, in its present context, the parable seems unapt or
inappropriate and when a more appropriate context can
easily be reconstructed, or when the parable seems clearly
maladjusted to its present context. Obviously this criterion
involves a high degree of subjectivity. A few examples must
suffice. No. 104, for example, is not unusual in being the
spiritualization or personalization of a parable that originally
applied to the historic experience of Israel. It is about a king's
son who is taken captive but eventually returns to his own
possession. Since the king's son is a standard metaphor that

normally represents Israel, it seems probable that this parable originally applied to Israel's captivity, exodus, and return to Canaan. But in no. 104, the only surviving version of this parable, it is applied to individual experience: "Even so, a wise scholar who separated from the words of Torah and then afterward walked according to them, if he is summoned to return, even though it be after a hundred years, he is not ashamed to return and face it, for he says: I am returning to my own possession." It will be noted that verbal adjustments have been made in either parable or application to create a closer verbal parallelism between them. (The reapplication of the experiences of ancient Israel to provide lessons for individual religious life can also be seen abundantly in Christian homilies!)

A case of very imperfect assimilation to a new context, proceeding by stages (as can be observed in the corruptions of the text and in the difference between the two recensions of Aboth de Rabbi Nathan), is seen in no. 26. One may conjecture that the parable was originally used in a moralistic context, and the textual confusion arose from attempts on the part of editors or copyists to fit the illustration better to the new illustrand.

Our collection exhibits examples that show the first stage of a new application hovering on the edge and threatening to replace the original one, which still remains. Thus in no. 57 we see immediately following the parabolic pericope the comment, "Rabbi says: This proclaims the excellence of Israel. . . ." If this is a secondary application, one can only say that it is a striking departure from the original one, which portrays Israel's reluctance to accept God's kingship until He performed benefactions for them.

Not only may there be some disagreement between the parable and its context, but it can sometimes be observed that there is a disjunction between the illustrand that immediately precedes the parable and the application that immediately follows it, suggesting that one or the other may not be original. In an anonymous parable in Sifre on Deuteronomy 36, not only is there some tension between the parable and its application, but there seems to be no relation between the illustrand and the application, each being essentially a different verse of Scripture.

"To the choirmaster: According to the *sheminith*. A psalm of David" (Ps. 12, superscription)

A parable. It is like unto a king of flesh and blood who said to his wife: Adorn and beautify yourself before me! She said: Why? He said: So that you may be pleasing to me.

Even so the Holy One, blessed be He, said to Israel: "You are beautiful as Tirzah, My love" (Song 6:4).

A more striking case is no. 98, where the illustrand indicates that the parable is about the sons of Aaron, who replace the sons of Moses. The application, however, indicates that the parable is about Joshua, who, instead of Moses' sons, succeeds Moses.

That reapplication has occurred is a patent certainty when a rabbinic parable is known to be an adaptation of a story that has earlier appeared in non-Jewish sources. If there is no question about the direction of literary dependence, there can be no question about the fact of reapplication.

At least three of our parables clearly originated as pagan fables or myths. Akiba's story The Fox and the Fishes (no. 18) is traceable ultimately to an Indian source, *Baka Jataka*, but he has applied it to a point that is quintessentially rabbinic; there could hardly be a more clear-cut or dramatic example of reapplication. The Wise Sheep Dogs (no. 84) appears to be a typical Aesopic fable. The Curious Wife and the Scorpion (no. 27) appears to be an adaptation of the myth of Pandora's Box, and the adaptation has been imperfectly worked out.

There is a striking similarity between some Tannaitic parables and some that are ascribed to Jesus. Thus no. 19 bears an uncanny resemblance to Matthew 22:11–14 and 25:1–3, and even their interpretations or applications are related. But if no. 68 is related to Matthew 20:1–16, one can only say that the applications are opposite! And if no. 114 owes anything to Luke 15:11–24, the point has been made simpler and more obvious. The direction of dependence in these cases is, of course, a moot question.

A considerable number of Tannaitic parables are found more than once in our sources. These parallel versions can be compared with a view to discovering whether they are always employed to make the same point, or whether reapplication has occurred. Such a comparison does in fact reveal a considerable number of reapplications, of which only a few examples will be given here.

The Great Inheritance (no. 86) appears a second time in Sifre on Deuteronomy. In the first version the inheritance is the Promised Land, literal Canaan. In the second version, however, the inheritance is the future life. This is a striking case of spiritualization, a phenomenon already noted. Most probably the first version is the earlier and original one.

The application is identical in all versions of The Escape from Three Perils (no. 39), but the illustrands differ. The version supplied in part 1 above illustrates the deliverance from the Egyptians; two other places make it about the war with Gog and Magog; and a fourth version interprets the whole comprehensively and probably gives us the total intent of the parable.

The Slave and the Rotten Fish (no. 40) probably exhibits the original context, which is historical and exegetical. A more elaborate version appears in Pesikta de Rab Kahana 11:3. While it retains there the explicit application, it uses it in connection with a different illustrand, Proverbs 7:10, thus changing its thrust to a personal religious one.

A striking shift of meaning in the Parable of the Wise and Foolish Invitees (no. 19) is revealed not only by a comparison of different versions but by a careful study of their contexts. In both versions the parable occurs as a commentary on Ecclesiastes 9:8 ("Let thy garments be always white"), but the context of no. 19 shows that the juxtaposition of illustrand and illustration is the work of editors, for Eliezer's dictum must be later than the parable of Johanan his teacher. (In the later version of Eccl. R. 9:8:1, the illustrand is ascribed to Johanan and the parable to Judah ha-Nasi.) Eliezer himself may have applied or reapplied Johanan's parable to the lesson: Always be ready for death. That was probably not quite Johanan's original point, which was probably: Always be ready for the coming of the messiah.

Our suspicions here are already aroused by the banquet in the parable, which is an obvious reference to the messianic age. Our suspicions seem to be confirmed when we compare the parallel version, which, unlike no. 19, has an explicit application attached: "Even so in the hereafter [*le'atid labo'*], as Isaiah declares, 'Behold, My servants shall eat, but ye shall be hungry'" (Isa. 65:13). The Hebrew expression usually refers to the messianic age, although references can be found in which it may be interpreted to mean the future life in a vaguer sense. Thus Johanan's parable (like those of Jesus in Matt. 22:11–14 and 25:1–13) originally had reference to the coming of the messiah, but Eliezer (or the Talmudic editor) reapplied it to the coming of death to the individual. The two meanings are, to be sure, congruent to each other, being two different ways of regarding entrance into the future life.

We may conclude, then, that reapplications have occurred. Sometimes we find the original context in which the parable was first born and employed, and other times we find it in a new context, where it may fit equally well or not well at all. Sometimes modifications have been made in it to make it fit; other times the modification is insufficient or even lacking. A parable is a picture that can be hung on any wall, but sometimes the colors clash.

If any trend in reapplications can be observed, it is probably in the direction of a more individual paraenesis— from national history to individual duty or destiny—and greater "spirituality." National sins are translated into individual sins, and national merit into personal merit.

8

RABBINIC PARABLES AND THE PARABLES ATTRIBUTED TO JESUS

Since both Jesus and the Jewish Rabbis made extensive use of parables as a major teaching device, it is natural to ask about the relation between these two bodies of material. An initial issue is that of the chronological relation of the parables of Jesus to those of the Rabbis. It has already been noted that the earliest rabbinic parables available to us are those attributed to the Schools of Hillel and Shammai and those attributed to R. Johanan b. Zakkai. Fourth Ezra, although not strictly rabbinic in character, is witness to the prevalence of parables in some Jewish circles about the end of the first century C.E.; as mentioned in chapter 1, in 4 Ezra 8:1–3 there is an approach to the dominant format that appears in later rabbinic literature. One may thus speak with confidence of the existence of rabbinic parables by the end of the first century C.E., but not much earlier. It follows that Jesus could not have been directly dependent on the rabbinic parables now extant, since he preceded them in time (his ministry was about 30 C.E.). On the other hand, it would be reckless to argue that the Rabbis developed their use of parables in dependence on the practice of Jesus. However many followers he may have had during his lifetime, it is clear that he became *persona non grata* to his countrymen, and it is psychologically improbable that the religious leaders copied his style of storytelling.

It should be noted that there are relatively few parables in the Jewish Scriptures, the Christian Old Testament, though one thinks immediately of the story told by Nathan to David (2 Sam. 12) and of Jotham's fable of the trees (Judg. 9). See also 2 Samuel 14:5–17; 1 Kings 20:39–42; perhaps Isaiah 5:1–7 and 28:23–29, plus a considerable number of passages in Ezekiel that are parabolic or allegorical in character (e.g., 19:1–9, 10–14; 24:3–17; 31:1–9). Proverbs also were a regular element in Hebrew-Jewish literature, and it may be argued that proverbs are frequently parables in embryo; that is, they could be developed into stories, and this process could turn them into parables. But clearly the widespread use of parables as a teaching device was a new development in the rabbinic period, a development only partially prepared for by earlier practice. It is safe to assume that the development began before our earliest documentation of it in the second half of the first century. Thus, however marked the parables of Jesus may have been by his own emphases, they undoubtedly reflect a widespread use of parables that had begun—or was beginning—among his contemporaries. While little more can be said about the issue of dependence, it is appropriate to investigate the similarities and dissimilarities between the parables of Jesus and those of the Rabbis in the areas of form and content.

INTRODUCTIONS

One of the most distinctive features of the rabbinic parable was the use of a tripartite introductory formula. There is no parable in the Synoptic Gospels that begins with this full formula. There are a few instances in which one of them is preceded by what has been called "genre identification." Mark 4:2, for example, says: "And he taught them many things in parables, and in his teaching he said to them: 'Listen! A sower . . .'" (with parallels in Matthew and Luke). Or Mark 12:1, "And he began to speak to them in parables. 'A man planted a vineyard . . .'" (with parallels in Matthew and Luke). But these genre identifications differ from the first members of the rabbinic tripartite introduction in that in the Gospels the identification is made by the Evangelist reporting the incident and not by the parabolist himself (i.e., Jesus). Matthew 21:33 is an exception, since here what is assigned to the Evangelist in Mark 12:1 is turned into direct discourse by Jesus, "Hear another parable. There was a householder. . . ."

Something at least resembling the second and third elements of the tripartite introduction does appear in the Gospels, for example in the Parable of the Children in the Marketplace:

> Matt. 11:16 "But to what shall I compare this genera-
> tion? It is like children. . . ."
>
> Luke 7:31–32 "To what then shall I compare the men of
> this generation, and what are they like? They are like
> children. . . ."

Significantly this parable is from Q material, and while the doubling of the question in Luke may reflect his redaction, the rhetorical question itself is clearly a part of the introduction used in Q. (The double rhetorical question appears in the Jewish Scriptures as a part of Hebrew parallelism, e.g., Isa. 40:18).

Again, Mark 4:30 begins with a rhetorical question followed by, "It is like a grain of mustard seed." The same structure with slight variation appears also in Luke. Matthew, however, begins the parable directly: "The kingdom of heaven is like . . ." (13:31). Similarly, in another Q passage, Luke 13:20 has "To what shall I compare the kingdom of God? It is like leaven . . . ," though the Matthean parallel again begins, "The kingdom of heaven is like leaven . . ." (13:33). Since the latter style is demonstrably Matthean, it is best to conclude that the Lukan version is the one that appeared in Q. This similarity, but not identity, in the introduction of parables confirms the hypothesis that the parables of Jesus and those of the Rabbis were developments off a common stem. The rabbinic form reflects a somewhat more developed stage, but it must be remembered that the Rabbis constituted a professional and possibly semiacademic group, while Jesus, in all probability, reflected the style of the lay community.

Other synoptic parables begin with a rhetorical question that functions differently from the second member of the tripartite formula in rabbinic parables. Thus Matthew's parables The Lost Sheep (18:10–14) and The Two Sons (21:28–32) both begin with "What do you think?" Luke uses the opening rhetorical question more frequently, but for him it has become part of the story itself and not just a preliminary introduction.

> Luke 11:5   Which of you who has a friend will go to him at midnight . . . ?

> Luke 14:28   For which of you, desiring to build a tower . . . ?

> Luke 14:31   Or what king, going to encounter another king in war, will not sit down first and take counsel . . . ?

> Luke 17:7   Will any one of you, who has a servant plowing . . . ?

In addition, numerous synoptic parables, particularly in Matthew, begin with "It is like" or "The kingdom of heaven is like." While this usage parallels some of the rabbinic parables that use only the third term of the tripartite introduction, it is not clear that the terminology is sufficiently distinctive to justify any conclusion about an interrelationship.

THE TRANSITION FORMULA

When an interpretation is attached to the story half of a rabbinic parable, the transition word is predominantly a Hebrew term that may be translated "even so," "so," "thus," or "similarly." In the majority of cases this is the term *kak*, which was derived from the earlier biblical Hebrew form *kaka*. In the Septuagint, the Greek translation of the Hebrew Scriptures, this term is normally rendered by Greek *houtōs* or *houtō*. In the synoptic parables, there are at least ten instances in which *houtōs* is used as the term of transition to the attached interpretation. To stress this point, *houtōs*, which occurs in all these passages, is here always translated "thus," even though the RSV and other modern translations sometimes use synonums.

| The Fishnet | Thus it will be at the close of the age . . . (Matt. 13:49) |
| The Lost Sheep | Thus it is not the will of my Father . . . (Matt. 18:14; cf. Luke 15:7) |

The Unmerciful Servant	Thus also my heavenly Father will do . . . (Matt. 18:35)
The Rich Fool	Thus is he who lays up treasure . . . (Luke 12:21)
The Lost Coin	Thus I tell you there is joy . . . (Luke 15:10)
The Servant's Wages	Thus you also, when you have done all . . . (Luke 17:10)
The Budding Fig Tree	Thus you also, when you see . . . (Mark 13:29 and parallels)
The Unclean Spirit	Thus shall it be also with this evil generation. . . . (Matt. 12:45)
The King Going to War	Thus whoever of you does not renounce . . . (Luke 14:33)
The Generous Employer	Thus the last will be first . . . (Matt. 20:16)

Ten out of the approximately forty parables in the synoptics is a rather low percentage, but it must be remembered that sixteen out of the forty either have no interpretations attached or, in two cases (the Parables of the Sower and of the Tares in the Wheat), the interpretations follow in a new context. Thus ten out of twenty-four synoptic parables with interpretations attached directly to the story use *houtōs*, the standard Greek translation for the Hebrew term most commonly used in the rabbinic parables.

THE ROLE OF SCRIPTURE

It has already been noted that Scripture played a prominent role in rabbinic parables. As we have seen, in slightly more than two-thirds of the instances, the parable is used in connection with the interpretation or clarification of a Scripture passage. In slightly less than two-thirds of the parables, Scripture quotations appear in the interpretations. If, however, one ignores the parables without attached interpretations, then more than two-thirds of the parables with attached interpretations include one or more Scripture quotations. Finally, Scripture quotations are exceedingly rare in the story half of the rabbinic parables.

There is a marked contrast between these statistics and those for the parables in the Synoptic Gospels. In only one parable in the synoptics is it introduced as part of an interpretation of a Scripture passage, namely, in the case of the Parable of the Good Samaritan (Luke 10:25–37). Interestingly, in this unique instance it is in response to a question raised by a religious professional. Furthermore, only one of the parables includes a Scripture quotation in the attached interpretation. In Mark 12:1–11 (and parallels) the Parable of the Wicked Tenants ends with a quotation from Psalm 118. On the other hand, the story half of three parables includes material apparently borrowed from the language of the Jewish Scriptures, although these are not in the form of explicit quotations. Note the borrowings in The Wicked Tenants (Mark 12:1–2), The Mustard Seed (Mark 4:32 and parallels), and The Closed Door (Luke 13:27–29).

Before drawing conclusions from this dramatic contrast, we must remember that a majority of the Scripture quotations in rabbinic parables are concentrated in documents that are essentially commentaries on Scripture (Mekilta, Sifra on Leviticus, Sifre on Numbers and Deuteronomy, etc.); the quotations are less numerous in other documents such as the Mishnah, Tosefta, the two Talmuds, the Minor Tractates, and Aboth de Rabbi Nathan. Even when these qualifications have been taken into consideration, however, it is obvious that the Rabbis made a more explicit use of Scripture in connection with their parables than did Jesus. Is it possible that the Rabbis were like some modern academics who are so addicted to footnotes that they cannot write or speak without them? Or could one suggest that while the Rabbis developed their thinking out of an intense preoccupation with Scripture, Jesus, as a layperson, was not so dependent on the literal texts of Scripture? Clearly there is little basis for judgment in these matters, and one must be careful lest religious bias dictate a decision in the absence of adequate evidence. A fair statement about the teaching of Jesus would be that he did quote from the Jewish Scriptures in his teaching, but the references do not appear to have been as frequent as might have been expected from reading the writings of the Rabbis. The fact seems clear; the explanation is a matter for speculation.

COMMENTS ON CONTENT

It is difficult adequately to compare the rabbinic parables with those of Jesus, since so many facets are reflected in each corpus. At one point, however, it is possible to recognize a clear contrast. In the rabbinic parables it is obvious that a dominant concern is the history of Israel and the practices of Israel growing out of that history. Roughly two-thirds of the parables fall easily into this broad area, even though the precise boundary lines may be subject to varying judgments. In the present collection see, for example, nos. 39–48.

The proportion of rabbinic parables related to the history and behavior of Israel is not surprising, since, after all, the purpose of the rabbinic literature as a whole was to affirm, interpret, and apply the experiences of Israel in the past to the contemporary life of the people. What is surprising is the apparent paucity of explicit reference to these motifs in the parables attributed to Jesus. The last sentence has been worded with considerable caution, since there is a peculiar problem in interpreting the parables in the synoptics. It is now widely held that the Christian community sometimes shifted the focus or target of Jesus' parables as they repeated them in the context of their changed circumstances. As it now stands in the New Testament text, the Parable of the Talents, or Pounds (Matt. 25:14–30; Luke 19:12–27), appears to be directed to individual believers who are warned that at the Parousia and final judgment, they will be called to account for their use of the gifts that were given them. In its original context the parable perhaps was aimed at the religious leadership of the Jewish community as a critique of their use of the opportunities their own religious tradition gave them. While the Christian community clearly *may* have shifted the focus of this or other parables, it is not an easy task to determine the precise thrust of the original, and scholars will certainly not be unanimous in their decisions. (For a classic study of this problem, see Jeremias, *The Parables of Jesus*.)

Other parables that might have had reference to the Jewish community or its leaders are The Two Sons (Matt. 21:28–32), The Closed Door (Luke 13:24–30), and even The Prodigal Son (Luke 15:11–32). The parable that most explicitly relates to the Jewish community and its leadership is the Parable of the Wicked Tenants (Mark 12:1–11 and parallels).

It begins with an apparent borrowing from the Song of the Vineyard in Isaiah 5 (the motif of Israel as the vineyard of God is deeply rooted in the Hebrew-Jewish tradition). It then stresses the failure of the tenants to respond appropriately to the owner and concludes with the killing of the owner's son. Doubts may be raised concerning the original intent and form of the parable, but in its present form it is unquestionably part of a polemic against the leaders of Judaism, as the Evangelist makes explicit in Mark 12:12 and in the quotation from Psalm 118.

Other parables that may with some plausibility be interpreted as part of a polemic against the people or the leaders of Judaism are The Children in the Marketplace (Matt. 11:16–19; Luke 7:31–35), The Invitation to the Great Banquet (Matt. 22:1–10; Luke 14:16–24), and The Unfruitful Fig Tree (Luke 13:6–9). If, contrary to the probabilities, all of these parables actually refer to the nation or its leaders, then there is a total of eight such parables—only a fifth of the total number. Striking also is the fact that insofar as these parables do refer to the Jewish community, they refer not to its past history but to the contemporary situation, which Jesus regarded as the time of crisis and decision.

Another comment may be made by way of comparing rabbinic parables with those of Jesus. It has already been stressed that the rabbinic parables were predominantly exegetical; that is, they focused on the received religious tradition and attempted to interpret, clarify, and apply that tradition. This focus was not characteristic of the parables of Jesus, as has been indicated in the discussion of the role of Scripture in them. The parables of Jesus, on the contrary, appear to have been heavily eschatological; that is, they were concerned with the anticipated future intervention of God in judgment and redemption. Obviously it would oversimplify to say that rabbinic parables were primarily exegetical while those of Jesus were primarily eschatological, but such a statement, while exaggerating the contrast, would be a helpful guide to the differences between the two bodies of literature.

A review of the forty parables in the synoptics indicates that roughly half were originally eschatological in one sense or another. Admittedly the evidence is not entirely unambiguous. It has already been mentioned that the early church sometimes shifted the focus of a parable by modification of the story, by the attached interpretations, or by the context in which a parable was placed. For example, in its present form the Parable of the Sower (Mark 4:3–8, 13–20 and parallels) is predominantly about the different types of soil, that is, the differing responses to the proclamation of the gospel message. Some scholars would insist that originally the parable was about the contrast between the insignificance of the sowing and the glories of the harvest, and that the harvest represented the time of final judgment or redemption, as was frequently the case in Jewish thought.

At the same time, there may be parables not originally eschatological that were turned in that direction by the early church. This could be true of the Parable of the Talents, or Pounds (Matt. 25:14–30; Luke 19:12–27), which in its present form seems to refer to the final judgment of individuals but originally could have been an attack on the Jewish leaders for their failure to make adequate use of the tradition they had received. (Certainly even on this interpretation it could have been an eschatological parable.) Despite these differences of opinion about individual parables, it is safe to estimate that half the parables of Jesus were eschatological—a marked contrast with the small percentage of such parables in Johnston's collection of 325 rabbinic parables. Yet this contrast is understandable, since the rabbinic tradition, particularly after the disasters of 66–73 and 132–135 C.E., was concerned primarily with the faithful appropriation of the inherited tradition, while the message of Jesus focused on the anticipated arrival of the new age.

Another item is related to this contrast between the parables of Jesus and those of the Rabbis. It has sometimes been noted that certain of Jesus' parables end with an element of surprise, an unanticipated finale. See, for example, the Parable of the Generous Employer (Matt. 20:1–16), in which the employer pays the same full day's wage to those who have worked only one hour as he does to those who have labored for the entire day. Some have argued that this element of surprise is inherent in the parable and that a true parable is a device to startle listeners (or readers) so that they are moved out of one world of thought into a new and unexpected world. While several of the parables of Jesus function in this fashion, it is a confusion of form and content to assume that this element is of the essence of a parable. A parable is a parable whether it opens up a brand new world for the listener or whether it simply illustrates, clarifies, or adorns a world long known. This understanding is important in the comparison of the parables of Jesus with those of the Rabbis. While the parables of the latter typically served to explicate well-known and long-established tradition, Jesus emerged, at least to a degree, as a dissenter and protester against aspects of the establishment. Inevitably, therefore, some of his parables had the function of opening up new vistas that he had seen, even though they were still in some sense related to the old tradition. Furthermore, as the proclaimer of the coming kingdom, he spoke of a new world and a new age, and this emphasis led inevitably to the introduction of novelty and a contrast between the old expected pattern and the promised new pattern.

VARIOUS STYLISTIC DETAILS

The King Figure

Kings are prominent in rabbinic parables, occurring in nearly half of them. In Jesus' parables also, kings appear, although considerably less frequently. The king appears in at least one version of five of the synoptic parables, and in six if one counts the section on the wedding garment (Matt. 22:11–14) as a parable distinct from the preceding story rather than a continuation of it. Just as in the case of the rabbinic parables, there are instances in which one version of a parable refers to a king while another version of apparently the same parable presents a less exalted figure. In the Parable of the Invitation to the Great Banquet just mentioned (Matt. 22:1–10), the Matthean version speaks of a king, while the Lukan version (Luke 14:16–24) refers to the lead figure simply as a man. In the Parable of the Talents (Pounds) Matthew 25:14–30 refers to the central figure as a man, while Luke 19:12–27 speaks of him as a nobleman who went to obtain his kingship. (This aspect of the Lukan version is often regarded as secondary, an element introduced with reference to the trip of Archelaus, Herod's son, to Rome to obtain the kingship after his father's death.) The other king parables are The Unmerciful Servant (Matt. 18:23–35), The Last Judgment (Matt. 25:31–46), and The King Going to War (Luke 14:31–33).

In three of these king parables the king represents God,

insofar as any specific identification is intended. In the Lukan version of the Parable of the Pounds, however, the nobleman who becomes king must represent Christ. In the Parable of the Last Judgment (The Sheep and the Goats), it is the Son of Man who is called king and who speaks of God as Father. In the Parable of the King Going to War, the king can scarcely represent God; rather, the figure is identified as a king because in that culture he was the one who made decisions about war and peace. However, in the last-mentioned parable, and perhaps in others, the point of the story may not hinge on the identification of the king with a specific person.

The Rhetorical Question

An examination of the synoptic parables produces only one instance of the rhetorical question inserted into the narrative but addressed to the listeners. In the Parable of the Wicked Tenants, after recounting the murder of the son, Jesus is reported to have asked, "What will the owner of the vineyard do?" (Mark 12:9 and parallels). Such a question parallels the rabbinic usage, though one notes that here the question is put in the future tense and the narrative then continues in the future tense, "He will come and destroy the tenants." In the version of this parable in the Coptic Gospel of Thomas, a gnostic writing, the story ends with the death of the son, that is, without the rhetorical question and the explicit reference to the punishment of the guilty tenants (though the following quotation from Psalm 118 that concludes the synoptic version appears also in the Gospel of Thomas). Still the rhetorical question does appear in this one synoptic parable and is a link with rabbinic usage.

In this connection we could cite synoptic parables in which a rhetorical question appears at the end of the narrative as an appeal to the verdict of the listeners, such as in the Parable of the Good Samaritan (Luke 10:29–37), "Which of these three, do you think, proved neighbor to the man who fell among the robbers?" or, in the Parable of the Two Sons, "Which of the two did the will of his father?" (Matt. 21:28–32). See also the Parable of the Two Debtors, "Now which of them will love him more?" (Luke 7:41–43). Reference has already been made to a number of synoptic parables that begin with a rhetorical question. Most curious in this connection is the Parable of the Servant's Wages, in which the story part consists entirely of a series of questions (Luke 17:7–10). Though not identical with the rabbinic use of the rhetorical question in the middle of the story, these instances reflect the same intention—namely, the desire to stimulate or maintain the interest of the audience.

The Rule of Three

The triadic principle is apparent in a number of synoptic parables. It is explicit in the Parable of the Good Samaritan (priest, Levite, Samaritan), in the three sets of guests who refuse the invitation to the great banquet (Luke 14:16–24; Matt. 22:1–10), in the three fruitless sowings in the Parable of the Sower (Mark 4:3–8 and parallels), and in the three sendings of servants in the Parable of the Wicked Tenants (Mark 12:1–11 and parallels). The triad is present but only secondarily so in parables such as the Friend at Midnight (Luke 11:5–8), Leaven (Matt. 13:33; Luke 13:20–21), and the Seed Growing Secretly (Mark 4:26–29).

The triads are at least as prominent as in the rabbinic parables, but again it is difficult to establish an objective criterion for determining when a triad is indeed a major triad. Furthermore, as in the case of the rabbinic parables, there are considerably more instances of a rule of two—at least the following ten:

The Two Houses	Matt. 7:24–27 (Luke 6:47–49)
The Children in the Marketplace	Matt. 11:16–19 (Luke 7:31–35)
The Unmerciful Servant	Matt. 18:23–35
The Two Sons	Matt. 21:28–32
The Second Invitation	Luke 14:21–23 (Matt. 22:8–10 is different)
The Faithful and Unfaithful Servants	Matt. 24:45–51 (Luke 12:42–46)
The Last Judgment	Matt. 25:31–46
The Two Debtors	Luke 7:41–43

The Rich Man   Luke 16:19–31
and Lazarus

The Pharisee and   Luke 18:9–14
the Publican

It may be only a coincidence or may be a factor of the limited number of parables, but there are no instances of the rule of two in Mark. Also in the synoptics there are some occurrences of a rule of four. The difficulty in determining which "rule" is being followed is evident when one notes that some parables listed under the rule of three could be listed under the rule of four. Thus in the Parable of the Sower there are three sowings that have extremely limited results, and this parable was cited as a "three." But actually there are four sowings—that is, the three poor sowings and then the fourth, which brought forth "thirtyfold and sixtyfold and a hundredfold." If one insists that the Sower should be classified as a "three" because of the three poor sowings over against the one good sowing, then it may be replied that the Good Samaritan parable should be listed as a "two," since there the priest and the Levite failed to respond, while the Samaritan met the challenge. A similar problem exists in the Marcan and Lukan versions of the Wicked Tenants, since they contain three sendings of servants and then a fourth sending (i.e., of the son).

As noted in connection with rabbinic parables, for purposes of contrast or comparison there is need for at least two persons or events, and three are necessary if some form of climax is intended. On the other hand, the principle of economy means that more than three or four items is undesirable or the narrative becomes unwieldy.

The Geminate Parable

In the synoptics the best illustration of the geminate parable is that of the Two Houses, which concludes Matthew's Sermon on the Mount (Matt. 7:24–27) and Luke's Sermon on the Plain (Luke 6:47–49). The same format is approached in the less familiar Parable of the Two Servants (Luke 12:47–48), but the construction of the two halves is not as parallel as in a typical twin parable. There are two other parables that with a little rearrangement would fit neatly into this same category: The Two Sons (Matt. 21:28–32) and The Faithful and Unfaithful Servants (Luke 12:42–46). Again, as with the rabbinic geminate parables, those in this category could be classified as wisdom parables. (Note that we use the term *geminate* for this type of parable because we wish to reserve the term *twin* for two separate but parallel parables such as those in Luke 15:3–10.)

The Element of Humor

When dealing with the parables of Jesus, it is as difficult to determine whether humor was intended as it was when considering the rabbinic parables. Those in the Christian tradition may have a tendency to read the parables too solemnly because of the halo surrounding the sayings of Jesus. But surely even an objective observer would have difficulty finding any parable in which the element of humor could be said to have played a major role. Certainly there are metaphorical sayings of Jesus in which the force of the statement is strengthened by the element of the ridiculous. Consider, for example, "It is easier for a camel to go through the eye of a needle than for a rich man to enter the kingdom of God" (Mark 10:25 and parallels); or, "You blind guides, straining out a gnat and swallowing a camel!" (Matt. 23:24). Yet even these sayings may have been intended more to prick the conscience than to stimulate laughter. We come to the same conclusion even if certain of these sayings were his version of accepted proverbs. (See H. Strack and P. Billerbeck, *Kommentar zum Neuen Testament aus Talmud und Midrasch* [1922], 1:828, 933–34.) It is probable that the intensity of Jesus' feelings reduced the propensity for humor, since humor is a characteristic more of a spectator stance than of that of a participant in a desperate struggle.

Series of Parables

Just as in the rabbinic literature, so in the synoptics, parables are sometimes bunched together in series, and— also as in the rabbinic materials—the arrangement in series is often the work of the editors and not demonstrably the parabler himself. Thus Mark 4 has three parables in support of the statement "he taught them many things in parables" (v. 2): The Sower (or, The Soils), The Seed Growing Secretly, and The Mustard Seed. In the parallel Matthew 13, there are seven parables. Matthew omitted, or transformed, the Parable of the Seed Growing Secretly but added five: The Tares in the Wheat, The Leaven, The Hidden Treasure, The Pearl of Great Price, and The Fishnet. If Matthew 13:52 ("Therefore every scribe who has been trained for the kingdom of heaven is like a householder who brings out of his treasure what is new and what is old") is counted as a parable, then there are eight and not seven in this chapter. Again, every one of these parables except that of the Sower is identified as a parable of the kingdom of heaven. In Matthew 21–22 the Evangelist brings together three parables: The Two Sons, The Wicked Tenants, and The Invitation to the Great Banquet. Probably all three were understood as relating to the struggle between Jesus and the leaders of his own religious community. Finally, Matthew 25 has three parables all dealing with the last judgment: The Ten Virgins, The Talents, and The Sheep and the Goats.

In Luke the most familiar series is in chapter 15, where three parables are brought together in defense of Jesus' aggressive concern for the religious and social outcasts of the Jewish community: The Lost Coin, The Lost Sheep, and The Prodigal Son. And there is another threesome in chapter 12: The Watchful Servant, The Watchful Householder, and The Watchful Steward (or Faithful and Unfaithful Servants). It is difficult to determine whether the hypothetical Q document, which is assumed to stand behind some of the teaching material in Matthew and Luke, presented series of parables. But it is practically certain that the Parables of the Mustard Seed and Leaven were linked together prior to their incorporation in Matthew 13:31–33 and Luke 13:18–21.

Thus the Synoptic Gospels shared with the rabbinic literature the habit of arranging parables in series around some motif. This tendency is scarcely surprising, however, since it is apt to occur whenever there is an extensive use of parables.

Animal Parables and Secular Parables

The Synoptic Gospels provide no illustration of animal parables (fables) or of secular parables. Matthew 5:25–26 (Agreement with Accuser) is something like a secular parable if it is taken literally, but in that case it is no longer a parable but a bit of prudential advice. In the Lukan version (12:57–59) it is probably intended as a parable calling upon persons to be reconciled to God. But if it is indeed a parable, then its meaning is not secular.

9

RABBINIC PARALLELS TO THE GOSPEL PARABLES

It may be helpful to list the parables attributed to Jesus in the Synoptic Gospels that suggest one or another of the rabbinic parables. The word *suggest* is deliberately vague. The link between a parable of Jesus and one from the Rabbis may be similarity or dissimilarity in the story told or in the interpretation derived from the story. If the rabbinic parables have already been quoted in part 1, they are referred to simply by number and, occasionally, some comment. (The synoptic parables listed here have the prefix *S*.) In some cases we have included quotations or summaries of rabbinic parables that were not quoted earlier, some attributed to Tannaim, and some to later Rabbis.

It may be helpful to repeat that practically all of the rabbinic parables in the extant literature are later than the time of Jesus, so there is no suggestion that Jesus borrowed from those available to us. It is of course possible that ancestors of parables in extant rabbinic literature were circulating in the time of Jesus and were known by him. On the other hand, it is unlikely that the Rabbis borrowed directly from Jesus because of the antagonism that existed between them and the Jesus tradition—although some borrowing might have occurred. Probably both Jesus and the later Rabbis drew on a common stock of metaphors and symbols.

S1. *The Sower (or, The Soils); Mark 4:3–8 (Matt. 13:3–8; Luke 8:5–8)*

While not actually a full-fledged parable, M. Aboth 5:15 is a relevant parallel:

> There are four types among them that sit in the presence of the Sages: the sponge, the funnel, the strainer, and the sifter. The sponge—which soaks up everything; the funnel—which takes in at this end and lets out at the other; the strainer—which lets out the wine and collects the lees; the sifter—which extracts the coarsely ground flour and collects the fine flour.

Each of the four metaphors is explained in terms of a certain type of scholar, only the fourth being fully satisfactory. See also the three types of Israelites compared with three kinds of nuts in Pesikta Rabbati 11:2, a passage ascribed to R. Levi, and the four types of fish (disciples) in ARNa 40:9. If the central thrust of Jesus' parable is the diversity of soils and is intended to encourage believers to be "good soil" bringing forth fruit, then the passages mentioned here are in a sense parallel. On the other hand, if the parable of Jesus has as its primary thrust the contrast between the three inadequate soils and the good soil, perhaps with an eschatological overtone, then there is little parallel between it and the wisdom-type sayings of the Rabbis cited.

S2. *The Mustard Seed; Mark 4:30–32 (Matt. 13:31–32; Luke 13:18–19)*

B. Taanith 4a contains the simile "A young scholar may be likened to the seeds under a hard clod; once he has sprouted, he soon shoots forth." The degree of similarity with the parable of Jesus depends on the interpretation given to the latter. Is it a parable about the growth and development in faith of an individual, as in the rabbinic saying? Or is it the growth in the world from the modest beginning of

Jesus' ministry to the final fulfillment of the kingdom within history or beyond history? Also, is the emphasis on natural growth or on the amazing contrast between the insignificant beginning and the final outcome?

S3. The Wicked Tenants; Mark 12:1–11 (Matt. 21:33–44; Luke 20:9–18)

At least since Isaiah 5:1–7 (the Song of the Vineyard), the vineyard was understood as a symbol of Israel as the people of God. Those responsible for the care and management of the vineyard were stewards for God, obligated to turn over to God the fruits of the vineyard. The failure of tenant farmers to fulfill their obligations to the ultimate owner was a common theme in rabbinic parables and discourses, and the motif was the same whether a vineyard or a field was involved. No. 101 is perhaps the closest parallel to the Parable of the Wicked Tenants, with the decisive difference that in the rabbinic parable the property is peacefully turned over to the king's son, while in the gospel parable the son is killed, as in the actual career of Jesus. As was so often the case, the rabbinic parable was interpreted in terms of Israel's past history, namely, the arrival of Jacob, who is identified as the son of the parable.

S4. Agreement with Accuser; Matt. 5:25–26 (Luke 12:57–59)

In the Matthean context this saying does not appear to be a parable but a bit of prudential wisdom, namely, Beware of litigation, since the outcome is uncertain and may be for the worse. In the Lukan context, however, the saying may function as a parable with the following implication: Just as you should avoid appearing before an earthly judge because of the uncertainty of the outcome, so you should guide your conduct with an awareness that you must finally appear before the heavenly Judge. In Pesikta de Rab Kahana 18:6 there is a warning against having to appear before an earthly judge where the outcome is uncertain. This comment is made in the context of a discussion about a financial debt. It then states: "But in the time-to-come, when a man owes money to another, he will say, 'Let us go and try our case before the king Messiah in Jerusalem.' Upon reaching the borders of Jerusalem, however, and finding within them an abundance of precious stones, and pearls of purest ray, he will take two stones and give them to the other . . . ," and so the debt will be harmoniously settled. (This picture of the future Jerusalem is a homiletical fancy, stimulated by combining phrases from Isa. 54:12 ["and thy entire border of precious stones"] and Ps. 147:14 ["He maketh peace by means of thy borders"].) The same material is repeated in Pesikta Rabbati 32:3/4 without naming the speaker. The parallel with the gospel material lies in the contrast between the earthly judge and the king Messiah, although the latter plays no real role in the affair.

S5. The Two Houses; Matt. 7:24–27 (Luke 6:47–49)

In the gospel passages the contrast is between hearing the words of Jesus and doing them. In rabbinic literature the parallel contrast is generally expressed in terms of the distinction between simply knowing much Torah and actually doing good works. This contrast is expressed repeatedly with varying metaphors, such as the two trees in no. 2 (structurally and conceptually very close to that in Matt. 7) and the four illustrations attributed in ARNa 24:1–4 to R. Elisha b. Abuyah (ca. 120 C.E.). The first two deal with the appropriate building materials and the proper order of their use if the new house is to withstand the rains and flooding. See also ARNa 22, in which R. Johanan b. Zakkai (ca. 80 C.E.) presents three contrasts: (1) if one is wise and fears sin; (2) if one is wise but does not fear sin; and (3) if one is not wise but fears sin. The three are then described in terms of a craftsman with and without the tools of his trade in hand. See also the metaphors in Pesikta de Rab Kahana 27:9, in which various types of persons in Israel are compared with various types of trees, their aromas and their fruits. Thus the tension between knowing and doing the will of God is a tension recognized in the Hebrew-Jewish tradition and has continued in the Christian tradition, frequently in the form of the tension between faith and works. The apparent contrast between Paul in Galatians and Romans and the epistle of James may be at least partially a matter of semantics.

S6. *The Lost Sheep; Matt. 18:10–14 (Luke 15:3–7)*

The Midrash on Psalms 119:3, commenting on that psalm's last verse, contains the following parable:

> As things go in the world, when a sheep strays from the flock or an ox strays from the pasture, who seeks whom? The sheep, the shepherd? Or the shepherd, the sheep? Obviously the shepherd seeks the sheep. So David said to the Holy One, blessed be He: Master of the universe: Seek me as the sheep is sought. . . .

While not in the form of a parable, Exodus Rabbah 2:2 relates an incident in which Moses ran after a small kid. When he found it thirsty and weary, "he placed the kid on his shoulder and walked away." Thereupon God determined that Moses was the appropriate one to care for his flock, Israel. Genesis Rabbah 86:4 relates a parable in which a drover leaves behind eleven cows and goes after the twelfth, which has gone astray into the Gentile area. The parable is in response to the question why Genesis 39:2 says, "And the Lord was with Joseph," as if he had not also been with the other tribal ancestors. The story is reminiscent of the Parable of the Lost Sheep, but the context is different. In all of these rabbinic parallels the quality of mercy displayed was that of past heroes of the Hebrew people, and their display of compassion and mercy is given as a reason for their elevation to positions of leadership. In the gospel of Luke the Parable of the Lost Sheep is one of three parables in defense of Jesus' concern for the tax collectors and sinners in first-century Palestine. The general principle is the same in Matthew 18, but the context in that chapter suggests the parable was there applied to the leaders of the fledgling Christian community, calling on them to seek out and bring back members who had fallen by the wayside.

S7. *The Invitation to the Great Banquet; Matt. 22:1–10 (Luke 14:16–24)*

See the Parable of the Wise and Foolish Invitees (no. 19 and the parallel), which is relevant also for the addition found to the story in Matthew—the account of the man without a proper wedding garment. Midrash on Psalms 25:9 reports the parable of a king who invited merchants to a feast but specifically excluded the artisans, until his steward pointed out that the guests would be unable to consume all the prepared food unless the artisans were included. Apparently the general point is that God's mercy is extended even to the undeserving, although the immediate application is to David who is cited as the psalm's author. There is a striking incident in P. Sanhedrin 6:23c (and in P. Hagigah 2:27d) about two pious men and a tax collector. The tax collector and one of the pious men died, the former being buried with great honor, the latter with shameful disrespect. The surviving pious man was horrified at this injustice. But in a dream he learned that his pious companion had been punished for once having made a mistake with his phylacteries and that his shameful death was in expiation. The tax collector, on the other hand, had once done a good deed: when the city dignitaries had snubbed his invitation to a banquet, he called in the poor to share in the meal. The story ends, however, with the conclusion that accounts had been settled; the pious man then went to paradise and the tax collector to fiery torment. A parable in B. Baba Kamma 79b asks the various penalties involved if one should fail to invite the king to a banquet to which the townspeople were invited, as over against a host who invited neither king nor townspeople (cf. Tos. Baba Kamma 7:2). The precise application of the parable is somewhat obscure.

S8. *The Faithful and Unfaithful Servants; Matt. 24:45–51 (Luke 12:42–46)*

A partial parallel is provided by no. 19, with its account of prepared and unprepared guests. Ecclesiastes Rabbah 9:8:1 repeats the parable just mentioned and then adds a second that may be more relevant. It is the account of a woman whose husband was a courier and frequently away. She was always attired in her best and when questioned responded, "Is it not better that he should see me in my glory and not in my ugliness?" Both parables reinforce the dictum that it is appropriate to repent one day before one's death, but since that time is unknown, one should always be ready.

S9. *The Watchful Householder; Matt. 24:42–44 (Luke 12:39–40)*

Note the parables cited above under no. 8, The Faithful and Unfaithful Servants.

S10. *The Talents (Pounds); Matt. 25:14–30 (Luke 19:12–27)*

Song Rabbah 7:14:1 recounts the parable of a wife whose husband had to be away for a time. He left her only a little money, yet she was so frugal and careful that when he returned, she was able to say to him, "See what you left me and what I have saved up for you. Nay, I have even added to what you left." Apparently the parable refers to the careful preservation of the Torah by Israel. Parable no. 31 in the present collection describes the anxiety of a man with whom the king left a deposit for a time, although the man had no obligation to increase the amount, only to preserve it. No. 58 tells of a king who provided different responsibilities to two administrators and comments on their differing responses.

S11. *The Tares in the Wheat; Matt. 13:24–30*

Genesis Rabbah 61:6 tells the story of a king who entrusted to a steward an orchard that contained two intertwined trees, one yielding life-giving fruit and the other a deadly poison. Confronted with the dilemma of caring for them, he decided to let them both grow and to allow the owner of the orchard to make his decision about them in due course. The story purports to parallel the dilemma of Abraham when he was called upon to bless the children of Ishmael and Keturah along with Isaac. (Cf. the same story in Midrash on Ps. 1:5 and Num. R. 11:2.) Genesis Rabbah 83:5 records a squabble between the wheat, the straw, and the stubble concerning their priorities, a struggle resolved only when the stubble was burned, the straw scattered, and the

wheat gathered into a stack where "everybody kissed it."
Partially relevant is Numbers Rabbah 4:1, about the king who
had many granaries, some filled with refuse and ryegrass,
although he was concerned only about the one filled with
fine grain. The parallel is, on the one hand, to various
idolaters and, on the other, to the Israelites (i.e., the fine
grain).

S12. *The Pearl of Great Price; Matt. 13:45–46*

In the Midrash on Psalm 28:6, R. Simon tells a parable
about a king who owned a single pearl, apparently of great
value. His son begs the king for the pearl, but for a time the
father refuses. Finally, in response to many entreaties, the
king turns the pearl over to his son. In the attached
interpretation the pearl is the Torah, the Jewish law, and the
son is Israel. After the Red Sea episode the people of Israel
sang praises to God and begged to be given the Torah. In
response to repeated requests, he finally granted the Torah
to Israel. In the Hebrew-Jewish tradition there were frequent
discussions as to why Israel was the sole possessor of the
Torah. Various answers were given, for example, that the
Torah was offered to all the other nations, but none was
willing to commit their nation to the required obedience.
Only Israel accepted the Torah as their most prized possession.

S13. *The Hidden Treasure; Matt. 13:44*

A wide variety of parables deal with the discovery of
treasure in a newly purchased field, or with the unexpected
find of an abundant water supply on cheaply purchased
land. The stress is frequently on the chagrin of the old owner
as he views the success of the new owner. In most cases the
parables are related to the chagrin of the Egyptians when
they realized what a treasure they had lost through the
departure of the Israelites. See nos. 41–42 and the parallels
cited there.

S14. *The Fishnet; Matt.* 13:47–50

ARNa 40:9 begins, "As regards disciples, Rabban Gamaliel the Elder [ca. 40 C.E.] discerned four types: the unclean fish, the clean fish, the Jordan fish, and the Great Sea fish." Each type of fish is then equated with a particular type of scholar, but apparently only the fourth type receives full marks. The passage occurs in a chapter presenting several fourfold classifications of students or disciples of the Rabbis. Unlike the gospel parable, however, there is not a black-and-white contrast but rather varying degrees of strengths and limitations in each category.

S15. *The Unmerciful Servant; Matt.* 18:23–35

Exodus Rabbah 31:1 provides a parable dealing with a borrower who forgot all about his debt for a time. Then when he remembered and confessed his neglect to the creditor, the latter responded, "Why do you remind me of the first debt? I have long since completely dismissed it from my mind." The parable is then applied to God and his amazing willingness to forgive. The interpreter goes as far as to say that when God notes that men do not repent, he nevertheless forgives them time after time. (Some editors of the text insist that the word *not* here must be a copyist's error, but the Soncino translation retains it.) While the initial interpretation of the parable centers on the astonishing compassion of God in forgiving sinners, the context of the parable is Exodus 22:25 ("If you lend money to any of my people with you who is poor, you shall not be to him as a creditor"). The interpretation then returns to this text in the concluding sentences, stressing the obligation to forgive the debt of the poor man or else face the judgment of God. At this point it parallels the parable of Jesus. Although the focus in Exodus Rabbah 31 is on forgiving a *financial* debt, this focus is derived from the Scripture passage, namely Exodus 22:25. In fact, this entire chapter of the document centers on the theme that those who have possessions must be generous with those who are less fortunate. Section 31:5 has a powerful statement on this theme: "When Israel asked God: Who are Thy people? the reply was: The poor, for it says, 'For the Lord hath comforted His people and hath compassion upon the poor'" (Isa. 49:13). The statement assumes the parallelism between the two phrases that is characteristic of so much Hebrew poetry.

S16. *The Generous Employer: Matt. 20:1–16*

Up to a point, no. 68 resembles the Matthean story, but in the rabbinic narrative the worker who received an unexpectedly large reward is said to have been exceptionally productive—the payment was actually earned. See also the parable told by Rabbi Zeira at the funeral of R. Bun b. Hiyya, who died at the early age of twenty-eight. In this parable the king spends most of the day walking and talking with one worker but then pays him a full day's wage. When other workers protested, the king tells them this one worker had done as much in two or three hours as the others had in the full day (Song R. 6:2:6 and various parallels). In Pirqe de R. Eliezer 53 (end) there is the comment that if an employer gives a zealous worker a full day's wage, it is no special merit to the employer, but if he pays full wages to a lazy worker, that is indeed an act of grace. The application is that Abraham, Isaac, and Jacob received their rewards on the basis of merit, but their descendants will be rewarded only because of God's grace. (See similar parabolic statements in the Midrash on Psalms 3:3; 26:3; 105:13.)

S17. *The Two Sons; Matt. 21:28–32*

Deuteronomy Rabbah 7:4 narrates a parable in which a king let out his orchard to two tenants for development: one planted trees but then cut them down, while the other tenant did nothing at all. It is then asked, "With whom is the king angry?" The answer comes: "Surely with him who planted [trees] and cut them down." The interpretation of the parable is that punishment will be more severe on one who learned the requirements of the law and then disobeyed them than it will be on someone who never even learned the requirements. Perhaps a closer parallel appears in Exodus Rabbah 27:9. A man sought renters to work his field. The first few candidates withdrew, saying the work would be too difficult for them. Then one came who promised to till the field, but he then let it lie fallow. The question was then asked: "With whom is the king angry? With those who declared, 'We cannot undertake it,' or with him who did undertake it but no sooner undertook it than he left it lying fallow? Surely, with him who undertook it." (Note that the owner of the field, originally identified simply as a a man, is now referred to as the king—probably an unconscious shift caused by the frequent use of a king as the dominant character, especially when this character represents God.) The application of the parable is that God offered the Torah to various nations, but they refused because the requirements were too difficult. Then Israel accepted responsibility for the observance of Torah. The thrust of the parable is that Israel's acceptance of Torah does not create privilege but rather produces a very special responsibility and the risk of special judgment.

S18. *The Guest Without a Wedding Garment; Matt. 22:11–14*

See no. 19 and parallel. See also Ecclesiastes Rabbah 3:9:1, a parable about a king who invited guests to a great banquet but required that each bring his own chair or other seating arrangement. Those who brought only wood or stones then had to sit on them, while others who brought more sumptuous arrangements enjoyed them. When those sitting uncomfortably on wood or stone complained, the king rebuked them for their impudence, saying they had only themselves to blame. Obviously the seats in the parable represent the actions performed by the persons during their lives.

S19. *The Ten Virgins; Matt. 25:1–13*

The Parable of the Wise and Foolish Invitees (no. 19 and parallel) is somewhat similar. See also the parable in no. S8 concerning the wife who was always beautifully attired so she could be ready for her husband's return, whenever that occurred. The Midrash on Psalm 10:2 includes a parable about a traveler who refused to turn in at a military post as night fell. Later, when he became terrified, he returned to the military post and sought admittance, but it was too late, and he was refused. Note also the parable summarized in no. S18 from Ecclesiastes Rabbah 3:9:1. Although the metaphors may vary, the motif of being prepared or being ready is common to many rabbinic parables as well as to the sayings of Jesus.

S20. *The Friend at Midnight, The Importunate Widow; Luke 11:5–8; 18:1–8*

See no. 16, in which R. Akiba is said to have told a parable to explain why God promptly sent rain after he observed a fast on behalf of rain, while a similar fast by R. Eliezer had no such result. R. Akiba felt that some such story was necessary, lest the general public assume that there was some major flaw in R. Eliezer's relation with God. The implication of the parable was that God answered Akiba promptly just to get rid of him as a petitioner, while he delayed in responding to Eliezer because he wished to continue the dialogue with Eliezer. Of course, all this may have been said partly in jest. In any event, its intent is radically different from the two Lukan parables. These two parables use the common rabbinic principle of *qal ve-chomer* in argument, namely: If *A* is true, how much more *B*. The application is that if even a sleepy friend or a corrupt judge will finally respond if one keeps pestering him, how much more will God respond if we persevere in prayer. Nos. 22–23 have some similarity with no. 16 but are not as helpful as parallels to the Lukan parables. The Midrash on Psalm 28:6 tells of a king who finally yielded to his son's entreaties and granted him a special pearl that he prized. But the application relates to God's granting the Torah to Israel following their songs after the Red Sea crossing rather than to the general matter of God's answering prayer in response to repeated petitions.

S21. *The Rich Fool; Luke 12:16–21*

In the Pesikta de Rab Kahana 10:3 there is an anecdote dealing with a wealthy man who kept adding to his store of goods but never paid the tithes required by the Jewish law. As punishment God sent madness on the man and destroyed all his accumulated goods. Here, unlike the synoptic story, the warning is against the failure to pay tithes and not against the dangers of wealth per se. The Lukan parable suggests passages such as Sirach 11:18–19 or Isaiah 22:13–14, although these are didactic materials not cast in parabolic form. There are also anecdotes in the rabbinic literature stressing the danger of arrogantly assuming the future is secure, when actually death is at hand. See Deuteronomy Rabbah 9:1 and the parallel in Ecclesiastes Rabbah 3:2:1–3. The Lukan parable, however, stresses specifically the dangers involved in wealth rather than in general human overconfidence.

S22. *The Unfruitful Fig Tree; Luke 13:6–9*

In Exodus Rabbah 43:9 there is a parable about a king who sent a tenant to turn an uncultivated field into a vineyard. The vines grew and produced grapes, but the wine turned sour. When the king ordered the vines to be destroyed, the tenant remonstrated, arguing that more time must elapse before good wine could be anticipated. The parable was told to explain why Israel engaged in idolatry shortly after coming out of Egypt, the point being that more time was needed for Israel to mature enough to produce good results. The thrust of the Lukan parable is not explicitly stated, but it probably meant that the hearers of Jesus were being given one further opportunity to respond and produce good fruit.

S23. *The Closed Door; Luke 13:24–30*

Note the parable from the Midrash on Psalm 10:2 summarized under no. S19 and the other materials cited there.

S24. *Building a Tower, The King Going to War; Luke 14:28–30, 31–33*

The two Lukan parables emphasize counting the cost of discipleship before making the commitment. And, as Luke 14:33 explicitly states, the cost of true discipleship involves renouncing all that one has. Pesikta de Rab Kahana, Supplement 7:3, contains a parable that stresses the cost of *not* being reconciled to God while there is time. A king was offended by the people of a principality in which he lived. He left the city and paused for a time some ten miles outside the city. A wise man then went to the people and urged them to consider the risks if they did not seek a reconciliation before the king went completely away from them. The parable was intended to illustrate the verse "Seek ye the Lord while He may be found" (Isa. 55:6). While this rabbinic parable stresses the cost of not being reconciled to God, the Lukan parables are close to the reverse—stressing the cost of being reconciled to God. In the total context in Luke, however, emphasis on the cost of discipleship was probably intended not to discourage discipleship but rather to encourage full and complete commitment.

S25. *The Lost Coin; Luke 15:8–10*

See no. 115, which closely parallels the Lukan parable, although in the rabbinic story the coin represents the words of Torah, while in Luke the coin represents a "sinner who repents," as is explicitly stated in 15:10. No. 111, the Parable of the Pearl Lost and Found, is applied to faithful Abraham, whom God "discovered" (a secondary application relates it to David).

S26. *The Prodigal Son and the Elder Brother; Luke 15:11–32*

See no. 44 (and parallels) and no. 114. While the latter story is less developed than the narrative in Luke, there is a striking parallel when the errant son is too ashamed to return to his father and the father says, "And is it not to your father that you will be returning?" Pesikta Rabbati 44:9 also has a story that suggests the Prodigal Son. When the prince complains that he does not have the strength to return to his father, the latter sends word to him, "Come back as far as you can according to your strength, and I will go the rest of the way to meet you." This is then reinforced with the words of Malachi 3:7, "Return to me, and I will return to you." (The story was told in a discussion about the ways through which the people could receive redemption.) Exodus Rabbah 46:4 has two parables dealing with fathers who initially rejected their corrupted sons but afterward relented. In the second parable the reconciliation is only hinted at, though made explicit in the interpretation.

S27. *The Rich Man and Lazarus; Luke 16:19–31*

Ruth Rabbah 3:3 and Ecclesiastes Rabbah 1:15:1 recount as an example story or anecdote the case of two men who were companions in wickedness throughout their lives. When both died, one joined the company of the righteous, while the other found himself in the company of the wicked. The latter complained bitterly at this apparent partiality but was informed that his companion had repented before his death. The parallel with the Lukan story is particularly in the conversation of the man in hell. He asks to return to earth for repentance but is told the time for that is now past, and this teaching is developed in a series of metaphors. For the contrasting destinies of the pious and the wicked, see the story of the two pious men and the tax collector summarized above in no. S7.

S28. *The Servant's Wages; Luke 17:7–10*

Though it is not a parable, a saying of R. Johanan b. Zakkai (ca. 80 C.E.) is appropriate: "He used to say: If you have labored much with the Law, do not claim merit for yourself, for it was for this purpose that you were created" (M. Aboth 2:8). In B. Kethuboth 61a there is an anecdote about two brothers, both Rabbis, but the one fed his servant after he had himself eaten, while the other fed his servant before he ate his meal. The narrative reports that Elijah came down and talked with the one who fed his servant first and himself second, but Elijah did not converse with the other brother.

10

VALUES FOR CHRISTIAN TEACHING AND PREACHING

Study of the early rabbinic parables affords valuable insights to Christians, especially to teachers and preachers. But teachers and preachers will likely perceive those values in different ways as they compare the rabbinic parables with those of the Gospels. Teachers and scholars may well emphasize similarities, while homileticians may focus on contrasts.

TEACHING AND SCHOLARSHIP

Readers of this volume will by now be aware that the parables of Jesus found in the Synoptic Gospels belong formally to the same genre as those employed by the early Rabbis. They will also have learned that this genre was produced nowhere else but around Palestine, apparently between the first and seventh centuries. The Palestinian parable is found attributed virtually to no one other than early Palestinian Rabbis and Jesus.

With few exceptions, apart from secondary citations, the parables of the Rabbis are recorded only in the classical rabbinic literature, and those of Jesus are preserved nowhere but in the Synoptic Gospels and the gnosticized Jewish-Christian work that calls itself the Gospel of Thomas. A few stray Palestinian parables make an appearance in 4 Esdras, a first-century work, and a couple of quotations exist in 1–2 Clement. All these works, except for the bulk of the rabbinic citations, bear witness to the use of the Palestinian parable in the first century.

It is fair to conclude that whenever we encounter a Palestinian type of parable in a literary work of non-Palestinian provenience, its real source must be elsewhere and earlier. Its Palestinian Jewish authenticity can be safely assumed; as yet no exception to this rule has been proved.

Once this point is established, some important consequences flow from it. While only a few score parables of Jesus have been preserved, a few hundred parables ascribed to the Tannaim (the early Rabbis) exist. This enlarged sample enables us to describe the genre with greater confidence and precision. We learn, for example, that it was not unusual for an explicit application to be attached to a parable, and that a Palestinian parable could have several tertia comparationis without becoming an allegory needing to be artificially decoded.

These facts cast serious doubt upon certain scholarly dogmas that have gained general acceptance since the publication of Adolf Jülicher's 1886 work on the parabolic speech of Jesus. Jülicher insisted that a good parabler need not explain the meaning of his parables and that a true parable has only one tertium comparationis, declaring that "half parable and half allegory is only a mythological being." (Paul Fiebig, through his early work on rabbinic parables, disproved the latter assertion, but he was not heeded.) Therefore the explanations and applications one sometimes finds attached to parables in the Gospels (e.g. Mark 4:14–20) cannot be declared inauthentic *on literary grounds*.

At the same time, the rabbinic literature displays the phenomenon of recycling or reapplication of parables, confirming the possibility that the early church or the gospel writers could have been inspired to do the same with the stories they had received from Jesus, in order to adapt them to the spiritual needs of their people. That would provide a model for Christian teachers and preachers to follow in later generations.

PREACHING AND DEVOTION

The Christian preacher will often be impressed with certain dissimilarities between the parables of Jesus and those of the Rabbis. At this point it is important to avoid the invidious comparisons made by earlier generations of Christian scholars that stressed the literary superiority of the gospel parables. Jewish scholars such as Theodor Guttmann and Asher Feldman have protested that such stereotyped contrasts are unjust, and in any case the two bodies of parables were differently transmitted. Both collections of parables tell of nature, agriculture, merchants, kings, and servants. To the Christian mind the gospel parables have more pathos and profundity, though the rabbinic parables are often clever, but these are perhaps subjective judgments. In respect to another point of contrast, however, we are on safer ground.

One of the most dramatic results of comparing the gospel parables with the rabbinic is the discovery that Jesus and the Rabbis used the same device for often quite opposite purposes. The rabbinic parables seek to resolve difficulties, but the parables of Jesus create difficulties. The parables of the Rabbis were intended to make life and thought easier, but those of Jesus made them harder. Above all, where the parables of the Rabbis were meant to reinforce the conventional values of the time, the parables of Jesus subverted those values, even turning them upside down. This "bolt from the blue" shock value is certainly not a generic characteristic of Palestinian parables in general, but it is a striking feature of those told by Jesus, and it goes a long way toward explaining why he was crucified.

This fundamental difference is seen most clearly when Jesus and the Rabbis told similar stories—or different versions of the same story. It is hard not to see some relationship between the Parables of the Exceptional Laborer (no. 68) and the Generous Employer (Matt. 20:1–16). It seems likely that the Parable of the Exceptional Laborer or something like it was circulating in the time of Jesus. It is perfectly natural and apt to its point, hinging on the reasonable principle that reward should be in proportion to performance. It is more natural to assume that Jesus adapted the rabbinic story than the reverse because his version is the more unlikely (the so-called principle of *lectio difficilior*). If so, it opens up a wide window of opportunity and insight for the Christian preacher.

What might a preacher do? The preacher can invite the audience to exercise their historical imagination and put themselves in the place of Jesus' first hearers, who would have been familiar with the rabbinic story. He tells the story, stressing its appeal to fairness, common sense, prudence, and everyday piety. The employer in the rabbinic story is normal and just. The preacher creates empathy with the original Jewish hearers of Jesus. It was hard to be a faithful Jew, especially of the Pharisaic persuasion—but it was worth it, according to this parable.

Having thus painted the mental picture, the preacher moves on to Jesus' version of the story, explaining the details. Only the laborers hired at the beginning of the day are told how much pay they will receive. One denarius was the normal daily wage for an agricultural worker, and it was just about the minimum he needed to support himself and his family. On less he could scarcely live. Those hired later were only told that they would be given what is fair. Against the background of the familiar rabbinic story, Jesus' hearers would have understood the various groups of workers hired at different times throughout the day to represent various religious categories of people, such as strictly observant Pharisees, Jews who were less religious (the Ammei ha-Aretz), publicans and sinners, Samaritans, perhaps even (as "eleventh-hour" people) Gentiles who turn to the Lord of Israel.

All is unexceptional until verses 9–10 of Matthew 20. At that point the story seems to go shockingly wrong! It suddenly takes an unexpected turn into a surprise ending about One who pays His servants not according to what they deserve but according to His own extravagant generosity. Comparison with the rabbinic parable clarifies and under-lines the full meaning of the gospel parable. It helps us to see it fresh. (One might go on to explain the relationship of Matt. 20:1–16 to 19:27 and the shift from the setting of Jesus to that of the Evangelist.)

We have become too well accustomed to the parables of Jesus. When we steep ourselves in the rabbinic parables, we can then exercise our historical imagination and begin to sense how his parables must have struck their first hearers, and we realize how upsetting they were. Jesus was a disturber of the pious. In their eyes he was too easy on prodigal sons and lost sheep. All people become angry when their cherished values are challenged, when their tidy world is turned upside down. A revolutionary should not be surprised to find himself crucified.

We have domesticated Jesus and tamed his parables. But rightly understood, his parables still shock. We will find it much harder to come to terms with them if we can hear them afresh. Use of the rabbinic parables, which are always so sensible, will help us to restore perspective to Jesus' parables.

On the other hand, the Christian reader need not think that common-sense piety is always wrong. The community must be preserved, and to this end, simple morality is not to be despised. A story such as The Foolish Shipmate (no. 113) has something to say to an excessively individualistic generation bent on "doing its own thing." The stark alternatives of the results of obedience and disobedience set forth in Deuteronomy 28–30 are personalized and individualized in The Two Paths (no. 96), which reminds us of an ancient truth as easily forgotten as it is well known: a course of life may be attractive and pleasant to start with, yet have a bitter end.

Finally, it is obvious that a very large proportion of these parables are exegetical; that is, they were devised to illustrate passages of Scripture. Many of them are still apt to that purpose and therefore useful or clever devices to illuminate Scripture, or at least to make it more interesting. Biblical preaching is not damaged by colorful narratives. In fact, much of the Bible itself is narrative. The simplest, most elemental, and most effective kind of explanation begins with the words, "It is like. . . ."

ANNOTATED BIBLIOGRAPHY

A number of books and articles dealing with the parables of Jesus give only a brief account of the rabbinic parables or otherwise take little note of them. The titles listed here, however, in most cases deal directly and extensively with the concern of this book.

Abrahams, Israel. *Studies in Pharisaism and the Gospels*. 1st ser. London: Cambridge University Press, 1917. Reprinted together with the 2d ser. in one volume, New York: Ktav, 1967.

> One chapter compares the parables of Jesus with the rabbinic parables (pp. 90–107). Taking up the question of historical relationship, Abrahams sees no need to posit any systematic dependence in either direction, agreeing with previous scholars that Jesus utilized an already-established genre, though some interesting examples are cited of rabbinic parables that are traceable to Jesus, if not to a source common to both. The essay is largely taken up with rabbinic parallels to gospel parables, but very many of the rabbinic items cited are not themselves parables. Abrahams is especially concerned to reply to the assertion that in comparison to the New Testament parables, the rabbinic parables are literarily inferior, know nothing of the open fields and real life, and are concerned with trivial themes.

Feldman, Asher. *The Parables and Similes of the Rabbis: Agricultural and Pastoral*. Cambridge: Cambridge University Press, 1927.

> A polemic against Christian critics such as Jülicher, Fiebig, and Buzy, this work assembles a valuable collection of rabbinic materials—"all forms of speech which contain either implicitly or explicitly the germs of comparison," including not only metaphors, similes, and parables but also allegories, proverbs, narrative and expository material akin to parable, and even some euphemisms. The items are arranged according to figure types, with chapters on the field and agriculture, the garden,

trees, viticulture, the fig, the olive, the palm, the nut tree, the thorn and reed, the lily, the myrtle, and pastoral figures. In each case the biblical background and usage of the figure is summarized, and then extensive examples of its usage are given from the rabbinic literature. Feldman provides a veritable encyclopedia of standard metaphors. The chronological span includes both Tannaitic and Amoraic periods. Unfortunately, references are often incomplete.

Fiebig, Paul. *Altjüdische Gleichnisse und die Gleichnisse Jesu.* Tübingen and Leipzig: J. C. B. Mohr (Paul Siebeck), 1904.

The first Christian scholar to exploit rabbinic sources systematically in order to illuminate the nature of Jesus' parables, Fiebig was the first important opponent of the theories of Adolf Jülicher. The book stresses the need for completeness of materials and unbiased selection of examples. It sets out an annotated collection of fifty-three items from Mekilta, though the items are not all the same in form and genre, including simple similes as well as narrative meshalim. The second part of the book undertakes a serious formal analysis of the rabbinic parables collected in the first part, trying to be inductive in method. In spite of its partly polemic purpose and its indebtedness to conventional categories, it was a valuable pioneering work that deserved more serious consideration than it later received.

Fiebig, Paul. *Die Gleichnisreden Jesus im Lichte der rabbinischen Gleichnisse des neutestamentlichen Zeitalters: Ein Beitrag zum Streit um die "Christusmythe" und eine Widerlegung der Gleichnistheorie Jülichers.* Tübingen: J. C. B. Mohr (Paul Siebeck), 1912.

Fiebig's second and larger book on the parables was not only an amplification and elaboration of his reply to Jülicher but also a reply to Arthur Drews, the materialist professor of philosophy at Karlsruhe who had written a popular book boldly denying the historicity of Jesus as well as the uniqueness or superiority of New Testament teachings, attacking both Jülicher and Fiebig by arguing that the gospel parables were all borrowed from rabbinic antecedents. Fiebig's earlier book had been unwelcome in the mainstream of German scholarship because it seemed to give comfort to the traditional allegorizing interpretation of the parables, it had been taken up enthusiastically by Catholic scholars, and it threatened the picture of Jesus as a sensible moralizer that was dear to German liberalism. Fiebig therefore undertakes to press his points more fully and to do so in the light of the continued debate. Besides expanding the earlier theses, this book expresses several new emphases, stressing the importance of oral tradition, insisting on the importance of understanding Judaic ways of thought and expression, and demonstrating the identity of style, expression, and modes of thought in Jesus and the Evangelists with Jewish modes. The first part of the book is an annotated anthology of thirty-six items drawn from a wide selection of rabbinic sources. The second part of the book is divided into a refutation of Jülicher's theory and a polemic against Drews.

Flusser, David. "The Parables of Jesus and the Parables in Rabbinic Literature" (Hebrew). In *Yahadut umekorot ha-natsrut: Mechqarim umasot* (Jewish sources in early Christianity: Studies and essays). Tel Aviv: Workers Library, 1979.

This chapter, pp. 150–210 in the book, is expanded in the next title.

Flusser, David. *Die rabbinischen Gleichnisse und der Gleichniserzähler Jesus.* Part 1: *Das Wesen der Gleichnisse.* Bern: Peter Lang, 1981.

In this highly original work, Flusser denies that there are any parables in the Old Testament and advances the hypothesis that the parable-mashal was a native Palestinian development from the Greek proverb and fable. An intermediate form was the *Gleichnisspruch* (parabolic proverb), which was a "half-developed parable," examples of which are found in Matthew 9:37–38 and in M. Aboth 1:3; 2:15–16; 3:16; they went out of style soon after 70 C.E. At first the parables of Jesus and the parables of the Rabbis were just alike, being explanations of human life and its meaning before God. But about 120 rabbinic parables were put to the new purpose of illustrating biblical passages. Flusser's reconstruction of the history of parabling is necessarily built upon a very slender foundation of fact, but his discussion of the nature of parables is often very illuminating, and he rightly distinguishes parables from example stories such as the Good Samaritan, on the basis of structure.

Guttmann, Theodor. *Das Mashal-Gleichnis in tannaitischer Zeit.* (Inaugural-Dissertation zur Erlangung der Doktorwürde der Philosophischen Fakultät der Universität zu Frankfort a. M.) Frankfort am Main: Hermon, 1929.

Only thirty-three pages of this dissertation were published in German, and the original copies of the dissertation all disappeared during the Nazi era. The author later published the entire work in Hebrew, making some minor omissions. See the next title.

Guttmann, Theodor. *Ha-mashal bitkufat ha-tannaim* (The parable in the Tannaitic period). Jerusalem: "Guild" Cooperative Press, 1940.

A Hebrew translation of the author's German dissertation, this work contains eighty-nine pages besides bibliography. It comments on twenty-four parables, whereas the German stopped after the first ten. There is a final chapter giving a résumé of results, lacking in the German. The book is well focused chronologically, but not thematically, being concerned with matters of form, history, biography, literary worth, and whatever other matters the materials suggest for comment. It was the first full-scale Jewish study of rabbinic parables since Ziegler and is broader than the latter's work in concern and more disciplined in approach. The book produces the most complete list of introductory formulas, including many that are not really parabolic, the purpose of which is to prove that Fiebig was wrong about "the stereotyped character" of these formulas. Guttmann shows that the parables of Jesus and those of the Rabbis are basically the same genre, allowing for translation. He finds Tannaitic parables superior to later ones, although they are typically less elaborate.

Johnston, Robert M. "Parabolic Interpretations Attributed to Tannaim." Ph.D. diss., Hartford Seminary Foundation, 1977. (Facsimile available from University Microfilms International, Ann Arbor, Michigan.)

This dissertation, done under the direction of Harvey K. McArthur, gives more detailed background for much of the content of this book. Besides a history of the study of rabbinic parables, the work analyzes and comments on 325 parables, provides a formal analysis of the genre, and makes a detailed study of the interpretations as manifested in illustrand and application.

Johnston, Robert M. "The Study of Rabbinic Parables: Some Preliminary Observations." In *Society of Biblical Literature 1976 Seminar Papers*, edited by George MacRae. Missoula, Mont.: Scholars Press, 1976.

A preliminary report of some of the findings that were expanded in Johnston's dissertation.

Lagrange, Marie-Joseph. "La parabole en dehors de l'Evangile." *Revue Biblique* 6 (1909): 198–212, 342–67.

Partly in response to Jülicher and Alfred Loisy, this long article surveys the parabolic genre in extrabiblical sources—allegory and parable in the classical writers, and the Semitic mashal. The article depends heavily on Fiebig's 1904 book, as well as upon Wilhelm Bacher (a modern scholar of the rabbinic literature) and Ignaz Ziegler.

Lauterbach, Jacob Z. "Parable." *Jewish Encyclopedia* 9:512–14.

An early encyclopedia article (1905) on rabbinic parables, limited to a statement about general content, application, and five verbatim quotations. It became the model for several similar articles. Joseph Jacob's article in the same encyclopedia (1:221–22) throws valuable light on another aspect of the rabbinic parables by including a table showing the sources of some thirty rabbinic parables of an "Aesopic" nature. Students interested in the rabbinic use of such fables should consult Samuel Back, "Die Fabel in Talmud und Midrasch," *Monatsschrift für Geschichte und Wissenschaft des Judentums* 24 (1875): 540–55; 25 (1876): 126–38, 195–204, 267–75, 493–504; 29 (1880): 24–34, 68–78, 102–14, 144, 225–30, 267–74, 374–78, 417–21; 30 (1881): 124–30, 260–67, 406–12, 453–58; 33 (1884): 23–33, 34–55, 114–25, 255–67.

Pautrel, Raymond. "Les canons du Mashal rabbinique." *Recherches de science religieuse* 26 (1936): 6–45; 27 (1938): 264–81.

A very original study brilliantly analyzing the structure of the story half of the rabbinic and biblical parables. Pautrel insists that the gospel parables are the same genre as the rabbinic parables, though more skillfully presented. He estimates that the number of rabbinic parables cannot be much less than 2,000, though he selects only about 150 to illustrate his method and results, without distinction between Tannaitic and Amoraic specimens. On the basis of structure, he classifies the parables into two large categories—closed and open *meshalim*—while acknowledging that there are imperfect and exceptional items. Pautrel generally supports the conclusions of Fiebig.

Petuchowski, Jakob J. "The Theological Significance of the Parable in Rabbinic Literature and the New Testament." *Christian News from Israel*, n.s., 23 (1972–73): 76–86.

This article was first presented as a lecture given at the University of Manchester in 1971. The author reviews much previous parable research and regards as mistakes both the allegorizing interpretation common before Jülicher and the imposition of Aristotelian categories after Jülicher. He appreciates Fiebig but holds that he was not sufficiently at home in rabbinic literature to warrant some of the generalizations that he had made. Petuchowski's main concern is to counter the invidious comparisons made by Christian writers between the rabbinic and gospel parables, which he sees as a modern phenomenon that arose from the necessity of maintaining the superiority of Christianity and Jesus in the face of declining belief in traditional metaphysical doctrines and the supernatural. He discusses the comparison of the two sets of parables with respect to authority, aesthetic value, and religious distinctiveness, concluding that it is wrong to use the rabbinic parables as mere foils for those of Jesus. A subsequent issue of the same journal (pp. 144–51) prints interesting reactions from eight scholars, both Jewish and Christian.

Rabinowitz, Louis Isaac. "Parable." *Encyclopaedia Judaica* 13:73–76.

This 1972 encyclopedia article does not greatly depart from the pattern set by Lauterbach, though it is somewhat more expanded. After the usual discussion of the rabbinic use of parables, three main types are illustrated: king parables, with several subdivisions; animal parables; and parables from nature, including parables taken from daily life.

Stern, David. "Rhetoric and Midrash: The Case of the Mashal." *Prooftexts* 1 (1981): 261–91.

Building on the work of Ziegler, Guttmann, Johnston, and Flusser, as well as his own work for his 1980 doctoral dissertation, "Interpreting in Parables: The Mashal in Midrash, with Special Reference to Lamentations Rabba," Stern essays a rhetorical analysis of the structure of the classical mashal and its function within midrash (homiletic exegesis). Though the work is in some places marred by unwarranted generalizations and misreading of secondary sources, it makes a useful contribution in its sophisticated analysis of the parabolic narratives into "motifs" and "motemes," showing by comparison of cognate meshalim that the rabbinic expositors were able to compose parables spontaneously by drawing on a stock of stereotyped elements—not only standard metaphors, but standard plots and subplots that could be recombined into new parables as needed, like so many building blocks. He agrees that the form of the mashal became increasingly more regularized and standardized as it moved into the Amoraic period.

Thoma, Clemens, and Simon Lauer. *Die Gleichnisse der Rabbinen.* Part 1: *Pesiqta deRav Kahana (PesK): Einleitung, Uebersetzung, Parallelen, Kommentar, Texte.* Bern: Peter Lang, 1986.

An exhaustive treatment of eighty-two parables found in a homiletic midrash (book of edifying expositions of Scriptures read on Sabbaths and festivals) from the fifth or sixth century. The parables are mostly ascribed to Rabbis considerably later than those in our collection. The authors are a young Christian scholar and a young Jewish scholar who were students of David Flusser.

Thoma, Clemens, and Michael Wyschogrod, eds. *Parable and Story in Judaism and Christianity.* Studies in Judaism and Christianity. New York: Paulist Press, 1989.

This collection of essays by various authors is the result of a consultation held in Lucerne, Switzerland, on "Parable and Story as Sources of Jewish and Christian Theology." The book is organized into three parts. The first part ("Ancient Parables and the Gospel"), with papers by David Flusser, Clemens Thoma, David Stern, and Aaron A. Milavec, deals largely with rabbinic parables. One paper in the second part ("Literary-Critical Reflections on Parable and Story"), by Lawrence Boadt, discusses the rabbinic *mashal*, and other examples of them are used in some of the other essays, as well. The *meshalim* cited are from both the Tannaitic and later periods.

Thoma is at work on a highly technical analysis of some thirteen hundred rabbinic parables. This work is the latest manifestation of a burgeoning interest in the Palestinian parable as a special genre common to early Judaism and early Christianity, and sheds light on the relationship between them.

Young, Brad H. *Jesus and His Jewish Parables: Rediscovering the Roots of Jesus' Teaching*. Mahwah, N.J.: Paulist Press, 1989.

This recent publication of a doctoral dissertation done under the direction of David Flusser at Hebrew University insists on the importance of the rabbinic parables for understanding those of Jesus and affirms that the story-*mashal* is a unique genre preserved only in the rabbinic literature and the gospels, a point of unity between Jesus and his contemporaries. The third chapter is a discussion of twenty-three *meshalim*, which are cited in full; eighteen of them are attributed to Tannaim. Throughout the rest of the book ten more rabbinic parables are cited in full, most of them Tannaitic, to illuminate parables and teachings of Jesus.

Ziegler, Ignaz. *Die Königsgleichnisse des Midrasch beleuchtet durch die römische Kaiserzeit*. Breslau: Schlesische Verlags-Anstalt v. S. Schottlaender, 1903.

This large work provides 937 rabbinic meshalim in which a king or kingdom figures. Its intention is to show how these king parables accurately reflected conditions during Roman times, for Ziegler believed that they all had reference to actual historical incidents. Ziegler declared that it was foolish to debate the direction of literary dependence between Jesus and the Rabbis, that parallels are to be explained by tracing them back to a common conceptual store of the Jewish people and to common parabolic coinage. Ziegler was politely annoyed at Jülicher's invidious comparison between the parables of Jesus, which Jülicher had described as natural and spontaneous, and the rabbinic parables, which had been pictured as arbitrary and artificial products of men with bookish dust in their lungs.

INDEX